Prod No.	100528
Date	02.12.19
Supplier	Toppan

T.P.S	280 x 250mm upright
Extent	256 pages text and illustrations printed 4/4 (cmyk) on 157gsm Gold East matt art paper throughout
Cover	Print in 3c with UV ink (Pantone black U and double hit white) + sealer varnish on 100gsm Hot Branded paper , ref 785 cumin grey
Binding	Thread sew as 16 page sections, first and second lined; square back. Cased in with printed PLC over 3mm greyboard
Ends	printed 1/1 (Pantone black U) + varnish on 140gsm woodfree
HT Bands	black head and tail bands.
	All copies to have individual shrink-wrapped.

FURNITURE IN ARCHITECTURE

THE WORK OF LUKE HUGHES

FURNITURE IN ARCHITECTURE

THE WORK OF LUKE HUGHES

ARTS & CRAFTS IN THE DIGITAL AGE

AIDAN WALKER

FOREWORD BY TANYA HARROD

OVER 400 ILLUSTRATIONS

Thames & Hudson

CONTENTS

FOREWORD

TANYA HARROD

Luke Hughes likes to use the phrase 'make it disappear' when it comes to his furniture. This might seem at odds with his admiration for the products of the 19th-century Arts and Crafts movement, characterized by revealed workmanship and powerful, often archaic presence. But although Hughes is a furniture designer who is intellectually and artistically inspired by John Ruskin and William Morris (he is a member, or 'brother', of the Art Workers' Guild, founded in 1884 by Morris's disciples), he views the movement's development into 'studio furniture' in the 20th and 21st centuries with caution. One-off bravura feats of furniture making – whether by the American Wendell Castle, England's own John Makepeace or the remarkable Irish wunderkind Joseph Walsh – would undoubtedly win Hughes's respect, but such work is remote from his own practice. Instead, he takes inspiration from the designer Gordon Russell. In the 1920s, living in the Cotswolds, Russell was a disciple of the late Arts and Crafts furniture magus Ernest Gimson. But by the 1930s he had moved in the direction of Modernist design and batch production using workshop machinery. As Russell observed retrospectively, 'The most urgent job of all was to teach the machine manners.'

In fact, Luke Hughes's particular approach reminds us that we are blessed (or perhaps burdened) with the term 'Arts and Crafts' simply because, in 1884, a group of reforming architects and designers, including the polymath designer and artist Walter Crane and the metalworker W. A. S. Benson, decided to create an alternative to the Royal Academy, deploring its exclusive focus on painting and sculpture. It ended up being called the Arts and Crafts Exhibition Society, but the initial meetings were held under the heading 'Combined Arts'. This phrase better describes what Hughes sets out to do when he takes up a commission. He works very collaboratively, bringing in other makers and allowing them agency and freedom, *vide* Gyorgy Mkrtchian's abstracted carved eels on the altar Hughes designed to sit beneath the Octagon at Ely Cathedral (page 66), the lettering by Richard Kindersley for the Supreme Court's library in London (page 132), and the double-dragon door handles by the Scottish sculptor Jill Watson for the Keystone Academy Library in Beijing (page 222).

Although 'Combined Arts' can mean decorative complexity, the furniture Hughes himself designs is marked by simplicity and, where necessary, austere grandeur. It is designed to last. The aim is for his furniture to be 'completely service-free in perpetuity'. Of course, Hughes began as a hands-on designer-maker with his own workshop. But the furniture and fittings illustrated in this handsome book are no longer made by him. From a craft point of view, he understands every step of the production process, but his designs are now subcontracted to be made in small workshops, mostly in Britain; the 24 tonnes of furniture for the Keystone Library in Beijing, for example, were made in some twenty such artisan workshops. Since 1990 Hughes has taken up a fascinating position, with an alliance neither to studio craft nor to the large-scale factory. Rather, he looks back to the myriad workshops used by the great 18th-century furniture designers. Indeed, one of the revelations of this book are the levels of skill that Hughes can draw on within the UK, aided by the Internet's speed of communication and associated digital design tools.

As a craftsman Hughes has a heightened sensitivity to materials, their strengths and limitations. Black walnut, for instance, is lighter than oak and therefore was chosen for the clergy furniture in the Sacrarium at Westminster Abbey (page 32), helping to protect its 13th-century Cosmati pavement. For the altar in St Giles's Cathedral in Edinburgh (page 78), Hughes made the bold decision to use a 4-tonne block of hand-tooled Carrara marble that sits on a smaller, thin slab of black marble, the shadow gap creating the illusion that the altar is floating in the sanctuary.

As these examples suggest, Hughes chooses to design chiefly for the public or semi-public places of worship, learning and work. Such places demand furniture multiples and sometimes the scale is huge – for example, the 1,500 chairs for the Chapel of the Resurrection at Valparaiso University, Indiana (page 106). Hughes has a special sensitivity towards ancient buildings, but all his projects engage with the ambient architecture, whether ancient or modern, seeking to honour the spaces that the architecture creates. As he points out, 'The building understands what the problem is when often the client doesn't.'

The building comes first. Hughes sees himself as a social anthropologist who approaches design problems and the production process with imagination and scholarship. He thinks hard about how people inhabit the spaces he is furnishing, how they will do so over the next hundred or more years, and how his designs can serve his clients' functional and economic needs. Some of Hughes's most elegant solutions are the product of the demands of multiple use – like his sculptural writing tablets for the auditorium in Michael Hopkins's Queen's Building, Emmanuel College, Cambridge (page 158). The tablets are removable, as the auditorium turns from an undergraduate lecture theatre to an auditorium or concert venue. Of the Theatre Royal at Bury St Edmunds, Hughes remarks: 'This beautiful Georgian building needed furniture that wouldn't scream for attention. If we got the furniture right, the economics of the theatre would work, which is a true undercurrent in all our projects. It's economic drivers that demand that benches stack or tables fold. Throughout our projects we are using furniture to enable the client to sweat the building as an asset.' Here, his ability to make furniture 'disappear' can be understood very literally. Hughes designs beautiful chairs, benches and tables but they are also demountable and stackable so his clients can achieve the flexibility to use an interior in multiple ways.

This attention to economic imperatives tackles head-on some of the problems that have dogged high-level craft ever since William Morris complained of having to work for the 'swinish rich' because only they could afford his furniture, carpets and wallpapers, or C. R. Ashbee wrote of 'a narrow and tiresome aristocracy working with great skill' for the wealthy. The split between the world of design and of craft in the 20th century arose in part because of standardization and the economics of scale. But thanks to the economic accessibility of today's technology, Hughes is able to combine fine craftsmanship with 'mass batch-production' using digitally controlled machinery. Thus, his Valparaiso chairs, meticulously re-engineered versions of the seating for Coventry Cathedral designed by Gordon Russell's brother R. D. Russell, have greater strength and better ergonomics than the original. They are made using sophisticated, digitally controlled machinery, but they still require the decisions and skill of individual craftspeople to select the materials and assemble and finish them. There is a special kind of modesty about Hughes's willingness to work with an existing artefact so as to honour a building contemporary with Coventry Cathedral, and a craftsman-like love for the task that guarantees this will never be a world where robots or artificial intelligence can take over.

Here lies the essential strength of Luke Hughes's approach. There is the probity of his designs and his pleasure at understanding a historic interior. He takes equal delight in working with such inspiring architects as Stanton Williams, Ian Ritchie, and Ahrends, Burton & Koralek, but he also enjoys refreshing less distinguished contemporary interiors. Above all, there is his admiration for his scattered workforce and its skills. Hughes does not rely on anonymous, unskilled labour working in automated factories. Instead, we can name Matthew Smith of Roland Day, Oxfordshire craftsman John Cropper, Wiltshire craftsman Richard Mouland, Alan Harvey and Trevor Ballinger at Fine Furniture Design, Joe Latta of A. Edmonds & Company of Birmingham.

The words of the great Arts and Crafts architect W. R. Lethaby come to mind. Asked in 1922 to set out 'What I Believe', Lethaby began: 'Life is best thought of as service. Service is first of all, and of greatest necessity, common productive work; labour may be turned into joy by thinking of it as art; art, thought of as fine and sound ordinary work, is the widest and best form of culture; culture is a tempered human spirit.' It might seem strange to see Hughes's furniture as in any sense 'ordinary' but I think he would like it to be so, in the sense of Lethaby's link between labour and joy.

Whether art or ordinary or otherwise, the work is fine and sound; and if such work allows everyday life to be lived with dignity and grace by those who both make and use it, then it tempers the human spirit.

INTRODUCTION

What makes a furniture maker?

It is no exaggeration to say that Luke Hughes, who has been designing and making furniture since 1981, is uniquely placed as the furnisher of British institutional and cultural life. Twenty-four cathedrals; 130 parish churches; the Tower of London; Westminster Abbey; more than sixty of the seventy Oxford and Cambridge colleges; the Law Society; the Institute of Chartered Accountants; the General Medical Council; the Royal College of Paediatricians; the Audit Commission; the Royal Institute of British Architects; the Institution of Engineering and Technology; the Bar Council; the Supreme Court ... The list of major buildings that contain Luke Hughes & Company furniture, and which together amount to the bricks and mortar of British society, both historic and modern, goes on and on.

To understand the social, familial, educational and economic influences that have helped create this energetic and hugely significant furniture designer, we need first to explore the two streams of heredity in his background. On the one hand, without any pretensions to nobility, Luke comes from the upper range of classically educated leaders of the traditional English establishment, the kind of people who occupy high positions in politics, the civil service, the law, medicine, science and educational and religious institutions, who recognize and respect their privilege, and who regard it as their duty or responsibility to use it and their accomplishments to serve society. On the other hand, his mother comes from a line of bankers – a clue, perhaps, to his business acumen, his iron determination, not to say stamina, to succeed, and his refusal to accept anything as a given without rigorous testing (he calls it 'bloody-mindedness'). Quite where his passionate commitment to working with his hands comes from remains a mystery, but there is no doubt that his intellectual rigour has been crucial to his work from the very first.

As far as that upper-intellectual-bourgeoisie impulse to 'give back' is concerned, Luke is nothing if not 'clubbable'. He sees himself duty-bound not only to join but also to steer (often financially) organizations of various intent and a wide range of aesthetic, cultural and political influence. A trustee of the UK Building Crafts College, he has served as chairman of the Mount Everest Foundation, and as a trustee of the Sylva Foundation, an environmental charity working to revive Britain's wood culture. He has sat on the Singapore Furniture Industry Council and, after twelve years, continues to sit on the Fabric Advisory Committee of Southwark Cathedral. He is a Liveryman of the Worshipful Company of Carpenters and a former Honorary Designer of the Worshipful Company of Furniture Makers. He was a trustee of the Artists' Benevolent Fund, and, for many years, was chairman of trustees of the Art Workers' Guild – the key founding society of the Arts and Crafts movement in Britain, with which Luke's own professional identity is intimately entwined. He has also served as chairman of the Grants Committee of the Crafts Council of Great Britain.

A long-time resident of Covent Garden, the once colourful and slightly disreputable historic theatre district of central London, Luke is also a member of the Garrick Club, the dining society set up in 1831 in memory of the man who revolutionized acting on the English stage, David Garrick. Its members are cultured, clever, creative, often anti-establishment and occasionally disruptive. His tendency towards, as he puts it, 'non-conformity in the pursuit of excellence' makes him an obvious candidate for such an organization, and his account in the club's newsletter of a plaque dedicated to members killed in the First World War in the club's entrance reveals his mildly exotic European heritage.

'The first name', he writes, 'is that of my ancestor (of sorts), Alfred Schuster [Luke's grandmother's cousin], killed at Ypres on 21 November 1914. His family story, a model of European bourgeois cultural and social mobility, could hardly be invented.

'One family branch fled Germany in 1811, after their Frankfurt warehouses were destroyed by Napoleon; another branch, after anti-semitism reared its head, left when Frankfurt was absorbed into the Prussian Empire in 1866. One of Alfred's great-grandfathers was a rabbi in Stuttgart; another was a son of the composer Carl Maria von Weber. A fourth was one

1 Lecture hall of the Art Workers' Guild, London, founded in 1884 and focus of the activities of most of the leading figures in the Arts and Crafts movement. The rush-seated ladderback 'Sussex chairs' were designed and made by Herefordshire chair-maker Phillip Clisset, not William Morris as is often thought.

2 Sam Schuster, great-grandfather of Luke Hughes's 'ancestor of sorts', Alfred Schuster, who died at Ypres in 1914. Sam was one of five brothers, all bankers, who came to Manchester from Germany in 1820.

3 Claud Schuster, later Lord Schuster of Cerne Abbas, Luke's great-grandfather and permanent secretary to the Lord Chancellor's Office for nearly thirty years.

4 William Morris, whose passion for the nobility of craft was the original practical force of the Arts and Crafts movement, and whose same passion fed his later embrace of Marxism and campaigns for social reform.

5 John Ruskin, pioneering Victorian art and architecture critic whose exposition of the human essence of craft and craftsmanship in the famous 'Nature of Gothic' chapter of *The Stones of Venice* formed the intellectual foundation of the Arts and Crafts movement.

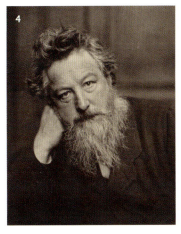

of five brothers, all bankers, one of whom, Sam, came to Manchester in the 1820s.

'A grandfather became surgeon to Prince Albert (and a pioneering mountaineer in the 1860s). An uncle (Arthur) was a physicist and foremost protagonist of X-ray technology. Alfred's brother (later Sir) George commanded a battalion in the Murmansk Task Force to Russia in 1919 and became finance minister in the Viceroy's government in India. A nephew became the poet Stephen Spender, whose brother Matthew was a pioneer of mountain-surveying techniques. One cousin Adela supported Oscar Wilde in his last years with a huge allowance (more than £250,000 in today's money) … Another cousin became Bishop of Cape Town. At least eight of them became Queen's (or King's) Counsel. One of them, Sir Claud Schuster (later Lord Schuster of Cerne Abbas), was Permanent Secretary to the Lord Chancellor's department [see the Supreme Court project, page 132], and while in charge of judicial appointments for almost 30 years, filled up its ranks as the nepotistic urge moved him. And not an aristocrat among them.'

As a finishing touch, aristocrats or no, bizarrely, and almost unbelievably, Luke claims descent from Nell Gwynn, arguably the most famous harlot of English history and King Charles II's mistress: 'She is my grandmother to the eighth generation.' She also lived in what is now Stukeley Street, barely fifty metres from where Luke's workshop was situated after 1981.

How did this richly varied and unshakeably establishment background produce a furniture maker, someone who adopts the traditionally inferior (in established social terms) professional career path of working with his hands? The link, unsurprisingly, is intellectual, and points directly to the Arts and Crafts movement, the result of the joint efforts of two eminent Victorians – romantic medievalist, designer and socialist campaigner William Morris, and art critic and religious revivalist John Ruskin – to combat the dehumanization of working people in the 'dark satanic mills', factories and furnaces of the Industrial Revolution.

The work of Luke Hughes is immensely, if not uniquely, significant to the English version of the Arts and Crafts tradition, and no other contemporary British designer or maker has an understanding of his place in that tradition as acute and as accurate. Luke sees himself as, in his own way, relevant to its continued vitality, and his relationship to it is one of the main driving forces behind this book. The proposition is that the true Arts and Crafts principles of honesty to materials and construction, and respect for the dignity

that Arts and Crafts was English and only English – the United States and various European countries all had their own versions – but here we are concerned with how a single craftsman-maker-designer can arrive at such a unique place in the history of English furniture. It is also not to say, of course, that Luke's work is restricted entirely to the English or British context; his Beijing office opened in 2019 (see Keystone Academy, page 222), and major installations in both the Far East and the US (see Yale University, page 178; Yale-NUS College, page 186; Congregation Beit Simchat Torah, page 98, and Chapel of the Resurrection, Valparaiso University, page 106) demonstrate that his rigorous but humanistic design philosophy is applicable the world over.

What becomes immediately apparent on encountering Luke Hughes furniture – whatever one may think of the design aesthetic – is its strength, its build quality and its longevity. It is nothing less than finely designed and finely engineered. We will return to this idea as part of the Luke Hughes process; now is the time to look at how it started, and to wonder, if not marvel, at the privileged and entirely academic education that Luke received, in which the acquisition of manual skills played no part whatsoever. In this respect, he is recognizable as an example of the 1980s phenomenon of the middle-class furniture-designer-maker, who may or may not – usually not – have had a technical education. 'There's something incredibly important about doing things with your hands,' says Luke, who wrote two very personal letters to his daughter about the roots of his craft during this book's gestation process, and which he has allowed me to quote at length. They are an eloquent expression of the excitement and fulfilment that arise from the physical, emotional, even spiritual engagement of the craftsperson with his or her tools, materials, processes and product.

Luke begins by wondering, 'How and why I became a craftsman, how on earth I learned some of the skills without any formal training, why I found it easy to float between the intellectual world and the manual one, and why I still find it essential to feel comfortable in both.

'One of my earliest memories, I could not have been much more than two, was when we moved from the

6 Luke Hughes & Company team member Luke Barton elegantly demonstrates the strength of construction needed for chairs whose hard-working life expectancy is fifty to a hundred years.

of the craftsperson working with his or her hands, are thriving in the work of Luke Hughes & Company, which itself is built around the engineering precision achievable by a superb craftsperson at a 'one-off' level, but which, at scale, needs the most sophisticated digitally driven machinery. Those who believe Ruskin and Morris were opposed to machinery as such have not understood their humanistic impulse. 'It is not this or that tangible steel or brass machine which we want to get rid of,' explained William Morris in an 1888 lecture, 'but the great intangible machine of commercial tyranny, which oppresses the lives of all of us.' What he hated was the alienation of the working man's process from his product, and the resultant degradation of human consciousness.

There is no doubt that Luke Hughes's work captures and expresses a quintessential Englishness – I do not say Britishness – that demonstrates that, at their very best, English design and craft are second to none. After forty years in which Luke has learnt, practised, experimented with business models and worked through turbulent times in business and technology, it is fair to say that his company is very much true to the spirit of Arts and Crafts, but a highly modernized and technologized version, which in itself provokes debate about the nature of craft. Of course, one cannot claim family apartment near Gloucester Road [in Kensington, the museum district of central south-west London]. Men arrived to take the glazed sash windows out of their frames on the fourth floor, rig up a pulley system so they could lower the enormous piano on to the street below and into the back of a truck to take it to the future home in Wiltshire. I was completely transfixed; buildings were clearly much more malleable than they appeared. And there were these special men who knew how to make them work. Amazing.

'When I was five, my parents began the works to rebuild and make habitable a ruined house at Old Wardour. Never mind the woods, lakes and adjoining castle (surely every decent house had all of those nearby!), for me it was just as much bliss to pad around the building site watching all the stone-masons, roof-tilers, plumbers, decorators and glaziers at their trades. [But] the real heroes of the site [were the] carpenters, Raymond (who had the specialist skills to build the bookcases in the library) and John, who did all the other carpentry work. I would watch them for hours, wonder at their scribing tools and honing stones, their clamps and saw-horses, their chisels and auger bits, their mallets, their try-squares and scribing profile gauges. They whittled away – sawing, splitting, planing, drilling, jointing. And it was not just the process of using the tools but the rhythm of their movements; where they positioned their feet, how they swung their bodies, tucked a pencil behind their ears, plucked their

chalk-lines, or even squeezed the splinters out of their hands. Papa took some advice from John and bought me some tools in a frightfully smart canvas carpenter's bag (I was perhaps six by then) and John made me a miniature saw-horse. The Cheshire Cat had nothing on my smile.

'When the house was eventually restored, we had other neighbours over the castle walls – the stone-masons engaged in removing the vegetation and stabilizing those same walls, making it safe for the public to roam around. There were a group of about seven or eight of them, all lazy, heavily unionized, and incredibly slow as workers (as is often the case with those employed by the state with no incentives). Nevertheless, over the years they quietly got around the whole building. They led the other masons, most of them involved with taking down the loose stones, removing the ivy and self-sown ash trees, and replacing them in new beds of mortar. Every school holiday I would watch them for days as they ingeniously moved the great stones about, how they wedged them against their squares and plumb-lines, how they back-filled with smaller stones, how they mixed and puddled and turned the lime and sand with just enough water to begin the chemical reaction but not too much to cause shrinkage and cracking, watching them flicking the stones with a wet brush to moisten the adjoining stones in order to draw in the mortar, watching how they split the stones or squared them up, how they selected them to over-sail

7 Old Wardour Castle's 14th-century stonework stands over the Hughes family home, restored in 1962 by Luke's parents. The 2005 extension to the right of the house is by Eric Parry, one of the architects who works closely with Luke Hughes & Company.

the joints or how they trued up the corners to set the bedding lines for the next course.

'After working hours, when they had all gone home, I would scamper over the scaffolding and the ruined walls to explore the rest of the castle and its curtain walls, squeezing through the tunnels and clambering over the turrets to dream about the rest of the building, trying to hear what those 14th century stones could tell me. I tried to eke out their stories – the mouldings, the mullions, the thresholds, the string-courses with their elaborate rose-cluster flowers, the interlocking winding steps, the flutings, the fire-backs, the lintels – letting my fingers trace the carvings and predict how the shadows they cast might change through the day. There, amidst this great treasury of stories, could be found the marks of the masons who had left these tales to be told; the identifying marks of actual individuals, members of a whole team of illiterate, itinerant geniuses, speaking to me from six hundred years ago. In those days, masons were paid by the volume of stone they worked; they could be left alone by the foreman for weeks at a time and when he returned to settle their pay, they had to be able to point to the section they had laid. Since they could not write, they marked the stones with a distinctive geometric mark – distinctive to them and the fellow masons – so there was no argument who had done which part. The castle has many such marks.

'But, like an artist signing a painting, their marks were also a mark of pride. The men had an identity. They were not anonymous, even after all these years.'

In another personal piece, Luke considers the influence of music on his love of making things. At the age of twelve he started sweeping up in the workshop of Michael Johnson, learning by osmosis the painstaking craft of a piano restorer for Broadwoods who went out on his own in the 1960s and became a key supporting figure in the revival of chamber music in Britain, building harpsichords for a range of early music specialists; later, Johnson shared his studio with José Romanillos, who made guitars for the renowned

classical guitarist Julian Bream, who lived locally and rented his barn to them both as a workshop. Johnson, now eighty-five, went on to become one of the world's greatest makers of harpsichords, with more than two hundred instruments to his name. Luke also describes the cello lessons of his early childhood, making the link to tools and 'manual cognition': 'I loved playing the cello. I loved the sound ... I loved the physical sensation of getting the instrument to sing ... I loved wrapping my whole body round the instrument, sensing the resonance and the harmonics through the woodwork ... a complex web of hands, eyes and heart. I also loved exercising my hands and arms independently of each other with the fingering and the bowing, and all the constant repetitions, the spacing and the co-ordination that eventually became fluent, ingrained and instinctive rather than merely painstaking or methodical.

'Many years later, I have wondered why I seemed to have such an affinity for using workshop tools, why it was that I so savoured the physical joy of making things, how it was possible to revel in the tactile nature of working with materials or the elation when it was going well, what it was that gave such pleasure to feel one's body flow through a workshop environment, the footwork, the balance, the smells, the touch, even the satisfying glow of tired limbs at the end of a day. I am now certain that any aptitude with tools that I may have stems from the neural pathways laid down through playing the cello from an early age.'

8 Man of many parts: like several of his Schuster forebears, Luke is an accomplished mountaineer. He can just about be seen here cutting his climbing teeth on the convenient 'climbing wall' of Wardour Castle, yards from his childhood home.

9 A 14th century mason's mark at Wardour, the signature, says Luke, of an individual member of a 'whole team of illiterate, itinerant geniuses, speaking to me from six hundred years ago'.

10 Michael Johnson, maker of two hundred of perhaps the world's finest harpsichords, in whose workshop Luke learnt his formative lessons of craft and craftsmanship.

Salisbury, St Paul's, Cambridge, the merchant navy, Morris Minors and the road to Covent Garden

The theme of craft and craftsmanship as a source of personal identity and its place in building and architecture continued through Luke's early education. As a fresh-faced, eight-year-old pupil at Salisbury Cathedral School, he was already fascinated with architecture, with the way buildings worked, the way that craftspeople interacted with them, and – true to the Arts and Crafts tradition – the way those craftspeople established and maintained dignity and identity through their work. What better example of great architecture's ability to lift up the soul than Salisbury Cathedral, boasting the tallest spire in the United Kingdom, whose ancient wooden interior-scaffolding still stands, and whose unusually short construction period – for the 13th century – of thirty-eight years guaranteed a stylistic consistency

unknown in Britain's other great ecclesiastical buildings. Luke's response to the building and its works is very clear in this section of his personal note to his daughter:

'I went to the Cathedral School in Salisbury, founded in 1092 and still housed in the 14th-century former Bishop's Palace. Never mind the music or the lessons, much more intriguing for me was the "cathedral works", into which I would peer to watch the inheritors of all these traditions. The cathedral building seemed – even to an 8-year-old – a sublime miracle, not just one of astonishing beauty but also of technical brilliance. Hundreds of thousands of tons of stone, mostly quarried very close to home but with even more ingenuity and gusto than by the masons at Wardour, hovering, shimmering, soaring, defying logic, treating stone like an ethereal cobweb: the columns, capitals and mouldings, the delicate volutes, the flying buttresses, the lierne arches, the complex geometric projections, the statues and porches, the complex lunettes of the cloisters, the textures of chiselled, carved and polished stones. And what of the spire itself? It still captivates and fascinates.

'Unlike the castle at Wardour, the cathedral building was still alive. There was glass in the windows, roofs over its intricate, formidable walls, bells that still rang, permanent bustle with services, ceremonies and concerts. Occasionally we were treated by one of the stone-masons to explore the hidden parts of the building (before the days of paid tower-tours) and on to the lead-lined roofs, which were being repaired at that time.

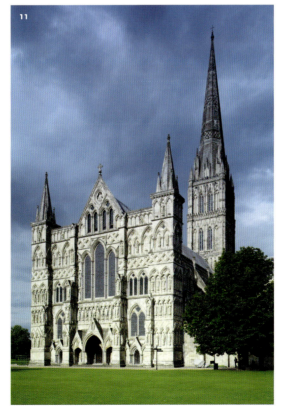

11 The west front of Salisbury Cathedral, with Britain's tallest spire looming above. At the age of eight, Salisbury Cathedral School pupil Luke Hughes found more to inspire him in the architecture than the music and lessons.

12 The young Luke was able to explore the 14th-century wooden scaffolding for the spire at Salisbury, completed in 1320 and still in place.

The plumbers laying the lead were allowed to add their "marks" alongside those of their predecessors. In the purloins and rafters of the roof structure, the marks of the carpenters who had erected them were still clearly legible. In later days, they had initials. In the early days, it was just their mark.'

The next step was St Paul's School, which in the 1960s had relocated from the City of London to Barnes, a riverside district to the west of the capital. It is to St Paul's that Luke attributes his talent for precise enquiry, but also the beginnings of his fascination with William Morris, the Arts and Crafts movement, and particularly its insistence on the dignity of labour, a principle that Luke holds dear to this day and which suffuses the atmosphere at Luke Hughes & Company. 'It was historical curiosity,' says Luke. 'Walking past William Morris's house [Kelmscott House, now the home of the William Morris Society] every day to the school boathouse made me keep on wondering, who *was* this chap called William Morris? Then later on I had a girlfriend whose parents seemed so proud to tell how their house was plastered with William Morris wallpaper, and when I got to Peterhouse [Luke's college at Cambridge], the dining hall had stained-glass windows, tiles and wall stencils by William Morris. Papa used to talk about Morris's books – he had a complete

set of *The Earthly Paradise* and a facsimile of the Kelmscott Chaucer [Morris turned to high-quality engraving and letterpress printing in later life].

'Even before I started doing history of art and architecture at Cambridge, I was already attuned both to William Morris and to his visual and technical ability. It's not insignificant that I found myself joining the Art Workers' Guild, not only because of him but because of all the others in that cultural stream: architects like C. R. Ashbee, Charles Voysey, William Lethaby, Basil Champneys, J. D. Sedding – members of that group that got it all going. This was before I made the connection about economics, how and why the Arts and Crafts movement originated, and what it was saying about society as a whole. I was very conscious of what it felt like to be a maker and being patronized for "dropping out". I chose to see it not as dropping out, but as stepping up, and fortunately I never suffered that kind of snobbery from my parents. My Pa said, go for it, no problem – but find in it that connection about the dignity of craftsmanship.'

Cambridge was, unsurprisingly, relentlessly academic. Luke moved from his history scholarship to oriental studies – revived, in 2019, in his return to the study of Mandarin and the opening of a Beijing office – and then changed again, this time to the history of art and

13 Blue Funnel cargo ship the MV *Atreus* in Hong Kong harbour in 1975. Shipboard experience gave Mr Midshipman Hughes's informal technical education a radically different direction from inlaying exotic veneers for harpsichords.

14 Family group in 1971, with Luke aged fourteen at right. Also pictured are his brother (left), Kim Nasmyth, now a world-renowned geneticist and biochemist; his stepfather, His Honour W. H. Hughes (or 'Pa'), whose surname Luke took; his mother, Jenny Hughes CBE; and his younger sister, Polly, who became a virtuoso violinist. His sister Jessica was in France at the time.

15 The Morris Traveller Reconditioning Centre, Bath, 1978, site of further lessons in the flexibility and durability of timber. Luke's own 'Moggie' sits to the right.

16 The first workshop in Lamb's Conduit Street, Covent Garden, London, 1980. Luke is working on his 'breakthrough project', the archive library of the Grenadier Guards.

17 No. 8 Stukeley Street, London, the old vegetable warehouse to which Bloomsbury Joinery, as Luke Hughes & Company was then known, moved in 1981; the lettering is by Bernard Jennings. In the 17th century, when the street was known as Coal Yard Alley, Luke's neighbour would have been Nell Gwynn, his 'grandmother to the eighth generation'.

architecture. It is from there that we can trace not only his own, very scholarly response to what he calls 'buildings of merit', but also the Luke Hughes & Company core brand idea: furniture in architecture.

But in the progress of Luke's (necessarily informal) visual and technical education, Cambridge was something of a lay-by. He had spent the year between school and university as a carpenter's mate in the merchant navy, crossing the South China Sea on a Blue Funnel cargo ship, the MV *Atreus*, and taking great inspiration from the Hong Kong Chinese ship's carpenter, Mr Zhang. Luke's adolescent summers in the workshop of Michael Johnson had introduced him to the finest work imaginable, all exotic timbers, laminated curves and inlaid veneers; Mr Zhang acquainted Luke with shoring cargoes and the lateral, improvised thinking essential to solving structural problems on the fly, all without the datum of a straight edge or flat surface and always under the threat of a listing ship in a typhoon. It contributed to the first-principles, enquiring mindset he learnt at St Paul's, and which he still values in the process of extracting and developing the brief from clients, who are often more comfortable with purchasing a product than expressing the precise nature of their problem. 'Extraction of the brief?' says Luke. 'It's more like destruction of the brief. Because clients are frequently asking the wrong questions.'

In some sort of proto-poetic fashion, the intellectual achievements of Cambridge were sandwiched between the MV *Atreus* and a wood-framed estate car. With a Crown Court judge as a stepfather, to whom he was very close, and many legal antecedents on his mother's side, it was more or less inevitable that Luke should gain at least some acquaintance with the law, which he did in a two-year course in Bristol after coming down from Cambridge. But his urge to work with his hands was insistent, and he eked out his student grant by working whenever possible on the restoration of Morris Minor Travellers, the 'woody' version of the quintessential British postwar family saloon. Again, no straight lines (or only a very few), and a solid foundation in various methods – machining, steam-bending, laminating – of achieving curvature in supple ash, the only timber suitable for this kind of work. Here was where Luke also gained the impetus to apply his overeducated intellect

(his words) to exploring the engineering properties of timber, its stress resistance and strength in compression and flexion, its 'bendability' and critical crack lengths or 'cleavage factors', which led in later years to the research he conducted in association with the engineering department at the University of Cambridge.

And so we arrive first in Lamb's Conduit Street for eighteen months and then, in late 1981, in Covent Garden. It is more than just the place where Luke set up his first workshop under the perhaps confusing name of Bloomsbury Joinery (Bloomsbury being the London district immediately to the north). Several serendipitous moments in the development of Luke Hughes & Company have occurred simply because of the magic of location, location, location; and it says something for the solid foundation of Luke's *haute bourgeoisie* confidence that he chose to set up in one of London's most famous – and expensive – central districts. The very first example of such serendipity was, as Luke recalls, 'purchasing in 1981, at a depressed price, a small vegetable warehouse in Covent Garden for use as a furniture workshop, despite knowing that notice of a compulsory purchase order had been registered by the Greater London Council ... then waking up one morning in 1983 to find that the GLC had been abolished – leaving an unencumbered freehold in the middle of Covent Garden (eventually sold in 2016 with a 1,500 per cent return).' There are definite grounds for believing that, in this instance, a man can make his own luck.

From Bloomsbury Joinery craft workshops to Luke Hughes & Company furniture designers, by way of the rise and fall of retail, a vicious recession, a manufacturing disaster and the ultimate creation of a reliable business model

From 1980 to the early 1990s, Luke Hughes and his workshop colleagues at Bloomsbury Joinery (in particular Mark Adams and Christian Jebb) made high-quality furniture for a variety of clients, mostly residential, but with the occasional foray into the institutional installations that are now the company's exclusive domain. Luke recalls how, in one of those serendipitous moments mentioned above, he landed the job that started him on the path to working for such institutional-based clients. Standing in line at the builders' merchant, waiting his turn to pay for tools and timber, Luke heard the plummy tones of the aristocratic David Gordon-Lennox, Colonel of the Grenadier Guards, one of the earliest (and equally aristocratic) regiments of the British Army. 'Anyone here put up some shelves for me?'

With the innate confidence of his social background, Luke was perfectly at ease both taking on work he had not previously attempted and engaging with what he irreverently calls '"OK yah" on steroids' (Luke's own spoken version of the Queen's English has more than a little plumminess about it). While everyone else in the queue stepped back, he stepped forward. The Gordon-Lennox shelves were a great success and led to the Archive Library of the Grenadier Guards. Indeed, many of the lessons learnt there are still being applied in such signature projects as the Supreme Court law library (page 132).

The real Luke Hughes & Company story of the 1980s, however, and one that brought with it many lessons, most of them painful, is the story of the 'Ovolo' range of bedroom furniture. It was at this time that Luke, who had already begun to write for *Woodworker* magazine on such subjects as the business aspects of a small craft workshop, was realizing that he had no interest in following the 'designer-maker' model, that of the (usually) middle-class craftsperson/designer

who 'was not making any money, and not making much furniture either'. He is dismissive of what he calls 'an RCA coterie', some of the furniture-design tutors and graduates of the Royal College of Art who 'might have had talent but just kept bleating that industry owed them an opportunity' – and this is where his business character, notably absent in the majority of his designer-maker contemporaries, comes into play. Not content with breaking his and his workmates' backs only to spend the small amount of money they earned on yet another set of expensive tungsten carbide-tipped cutters, Luke was searching for the acknowledged best-case business model, in which custom one-off jobs are supported by producing and selling a range of standard items. But that needed quantity production, and a sales force.

Which might well have walked through the door (location again) in 1985, in the person of businessman and management consultant Adrian Bridgewater (father of Emma, the ceramicist), who was working with the Midlands-based reproduction-furniture manufacturer Juckes Ltd, now long defunct. Their uninspired range was failing to keep them afloat, even though the late-1980s recession in British markets generated by Margaret Thatcher's monetarist policies had not yet started to bite, and the consultant was looking for new products and new ranges to revive the company's fortunes. 'He walked into the workshop', remembers Luke, 'and said, "I think you could design for this factory. Come and meet them in Birmingham."

'"I don't want to design repro mirrors," I replied, and he said, "Well, why not design something which the competition is not doing?" So I went to meet them, and started design development for them, coming up with a completely new range based on 17th-century Quaker furniture and very much inspired by the Arts and Crafts tradition. Victor Chinnery's book *Oak Furniture: The British Tradition* [1986] was a core text for me in this process. And so using those principles and what I already knew about production design, we evolved a design language for products they could easily make.

'But they were useless at selling it. So I personally started knocking on doors at premium furniture and department stores in London like John Lewis, Liberty's

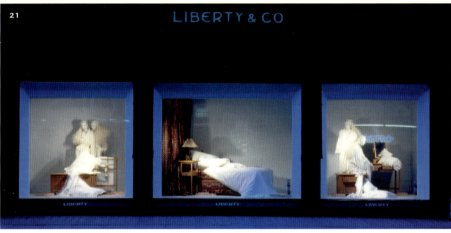

18 The Bloomsbury Joinery team in Stukeley Street, 1983. From left: Christian Jebb, Joss Skottowe, Mark Adams, Luke Hughes.

19 An elegant console table and mirror combination from 1983, originally designed for Chelsea Crafts Fair. The table's underframe is based on the balustrades of the Bernini colonnade in St Peter's Square, Rome.

20 The Notery from 1986, a stand-up desk playing a visual pun on 'notary'. 'In my view,' says Luke, 'people should be standing when doing small things.'

21/22 Major moment of 'arrival' for Luke Hughes & Company: the Ovolo furniture collection in eleven of the twelve Liberty's Regent Street windows, and a studio shot of the robust and modestly priced bedroom furniture. Production problems, copyright infringement and the late-1980s UK recession all conspired against the continuing success of the collection.

and Heal's. I remember walking up Regent Street in 1987 to find eleven of the twelve shop windows at Liberty's displaying the new Ovolo bedroom collection that had been designed and prototyped only six months earlier. Juckes couldn't believe it, and I confess I thought I had really arrived.

'But Juckes couldn't make to the required quality, so the pieces kept being returned. We were constantly being let down by the factory. It was also at that time that I realized that delivering a wardrobe to the John Lewis department store on Oxford Street [London's main shopping district] on a busy Friday afternoon was wasting time and burning up my margin in diesel and traffic jams. So I started looking for other outlets for the range.'

Here is where a major theme of the modern Luke Hughes & Company – the relationship with architects and architecture – began to take shape. An architect working for Britain's biggest chemical company, ICI, saw the Ovolo range in John Lewis, and decided it was perfect for the company's management-training centre he had just designed, where residential courses demanded well-mannered, sturdy, durable yet modestly priced bedroom furniture. An order for sixty bedroom suites soon followed, and having found other suppliers than Juckes, Luke Hughes & Company enjoyed a brief

spell in the sun making Ovolo for a string of similar training centres, including those serving Courage Breweries and Boots the Chemists.

But they flew too close to that very sun. Luke Hughes & Company had been officially founded in 1986, and in 1987, says Luke, 'I thought we were doing rather well, but we needed investment. So I approached venture capitalists, who showed me the door in less than polite terms. One of them, Charles Breese, actually came round to the workshop to deliver the same less-than-polite message in person – and he is still on the board, thirty years later. He knew a thing or two about raising money, so we raised an initial slug of £30,000 working capital, then in 1989 raised £300,000, almost all of which went into our own factory workshop in Tisbury, Wiltshire, near my home.'

That money was raised in November 1989. By the summer of 1990, the market had collapsed. There were no more management-training centres being built or furnished any more than there were consumers buying bedroom suites at retail. It was a wasteland. The Tisbury workshop struggled on for two years and closed in 1992.

It was a very low point, but like many low points it signified the start of an upward trajectory that has continued ever since, in business, craft and design terms. The key figure here is Ray Leigh, whom Luke – at

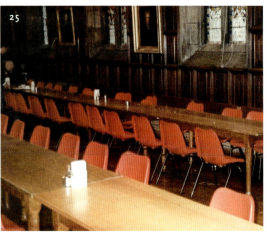

23 Ray Leigh, founding chairman of Luke Hughes & Company from 1990, and pivotal figure in shaping the strategy that created the company as it is today. An architect from the Festival of Britain generation, Ray was also design director, managing director and eventually chairman of Gordon Russell Ltd, arguably the leading furniture company to marry the Arts and Crafts spirit with design for modern industrial production.

24 Dick Russell (brother of Gordon Russell), the architect in whose practice Ray Leigh worked, and designer of the original Coventry chair for Coventry Cathedral, an icon of mid-20th-century British furniture design. It was re-engineered for the Chapel of the Resurrection at Valparaiso University, Indiana (page 106).

25/26 Before and after Luke Hughes: the dining hall of Corpus Christi College, Cambridge, in 1990 and 1991. Oxbridge was just waking up to the necessity for chairs instead of benches to attract the conference trade, but Robin Day's famous 'Polyside' moulded polypropylene design from 1963 was woefully inappropriate for the 14th-century hall.

the suggestion of Charles Breese, his first non-executive director – had invited to become chairman of the company in 1990. They had first met when Ray, as Master of the Worshipful Company of Furniture Makers, had been chair of the judges of a young designers' competition that Luke had won. Ray's track record as an architect of the Festival of Britain generation who had worked with Dick Russell, designer of the iconic Coventry Cathedral chair (page 106) and brother of the furniture designer and manufacturer Gordon Russell, provided exactly the right combination of production, design and marketing experience of which the fledgling – and struggling – Luke Hughes & Company was in short supply. 'Ray revealed he'd been design director, managing director and then chairman of Gordon Russell Ltd, the company that was probably one of my biggest influences, and he liked what we were trying to do,' says Luke. Thirty years on, he considers the sprightly, ninety-two-year-old Ray a firm friend.

'Ray opened up a whole new world for us,' observes Luke, 'the world I had been trying to get in front of for some time – designers, architects, manufacturers – and he represented a live link back to the Cotswold Movement and thereby the original Arts and Crafts designers and makers: Ernest Gimson, Ashbee and the Barnsleys [Sidney, Ernest and Edward]. As an architect,

he completely understood the link between architecture and furniture design. I would get an idea about something I wanted to do to push the company forward, and from his vast experience he would just gently and kindly say, "I wouldn't do that if I were you."'

When it came to Tisbury and the factory workshop that had already turned into a millstone, continues Luke, 'Ray said, "You're mad to do it yourselves. Why not subcontract? There's spare capacity in the industry, and you'll always get to use the right machine for the job." Charles asked, "Why don't we look at the sort of clients who survive recessions?" I said, "Well, Oxford and Cambridge colleges have survived five hundred years or more, and they all have one thing in common – buildings that they can't move around. They are all chasing the conference market [see 'A Tale of Three Colleges', page 166], and they have to be looking at better-quality dining furniture and bedroom accommodation."

'We knocked on a few doors and picked up our first job for Corpus Christi College Cambridge, then the Downing College library for architect Quinlan Terry, and then a vast job – worth £250,000 – for Merton College Oxford.' It was the start of the targeted business model that Luke Hughes & Company pursues, with increasing success and now internationally, to the present day.

27 Sir Philip Dowson, founding partner of architects Arup Associates, family friend and vocal critic of architect-designed furniture.

28 Philip Powell (left) and Hidalgo Moya, of 1950s Modernist 'starchitects' Powell & Moya, in front of their astonishing 'Skylon' space-age symbol of the 1951 Festival of Britain. The catalogue is pictured in fig. 29. Powell was another early influence on Luke Hughes's fruitful collaborations with architects.

Furniture in Architecture

The 'core proposition' of the Luke Hughes brand is 'Furniture in Architecture'. Although the company had been working expressly on those lines since the early 1990s, it was in 2013 – with the help of Craig Allen, former creative director at Linley Furniture and a senior buyer at the Conran Shop – that its brand messages were enshrined.

Truth to tell, it is Luke Hughes's relationships with architects, as well as with architecture, that have proved to be important in the development of this overriding company philosophy. It is also true to say, as we have seen, that Luke's response to architecture goes back to his very earliest years, the six-year-old enthusiast scampering up and down the Wardour Castle scaffolding. Perhaps the earliest significant relationship was with Sir Philip Dowson, a founding partner of Arup Associates, president of the Royal Academy of Arts in 1993, and a family friend. 'We knew the family very well,' says Luke. 'Philip never stopped talking. He was fascinated that I was going into furniture, and frequently came to the workshop (which was quite close to Arup's offices in Fitzroy Square), saying that I really ought to think about the struggles that architects have to go through to find suitable furniture to fit their buildings.' Dowson was refreshingly honest about architects' inability to design furniture, quoting his own attempts to furnish his Leckhampton accommodation block for Corpus Christi College, Cambridge, as 'looking awful'.

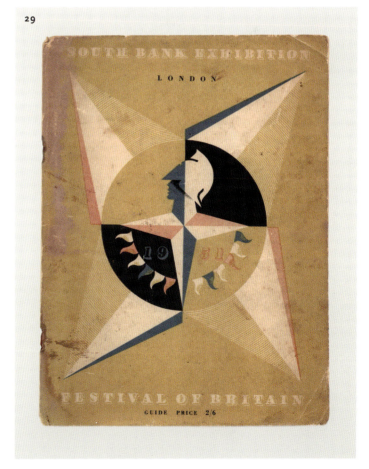

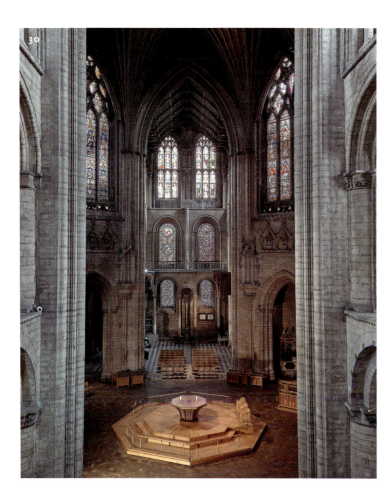

30 The crossing at Ely Cathedral (page 66) underneath the awe-inspiring Octagon, showing the new moveable altar, plinth and clergy seating by Luke Hughes & Company.

The next significant architect was another Philip, Philip Powell of Powell & Moya, whose reputation will rest for ever on the 'Skylon', the astonishing 90-metre-high (300 ft) cigar-shaped space-age symbol of the 1951 Festival of Britain, with which Ray Leigh had also been involved as a young architect. Powell's wife Philippa, director of the Chelsea Crafts Fair, invited Luke to exhibit, which he did during the mid-1980s, much to the interest of Powell, who visited the stand and then the Covent Garden workshop. A friend and contemporary of Philip Dowson, Powell's theme was the same: the difficulty of finding the right furniture for the practice's buildings. He was dismissive, for instance, of the furniture chosen by the client team for the Cripps Building at St John's College, Cambridge, a Powell & Moya project of the 1960s. 'He thought it was a heap of junk: five different types of furniture,' says Luke. 'For him, the whole point was that the architecture, interiors and furniture should make a seamless, integrated whole. The only company they liked to use was Gordon Russell, yet the client thought they were too expensive. He wagged a finger at me and said, "If you can get your thinking round furnishing in the manner of the building, you will never be out of work."'

So much for the Modernists. But a high proportion of Luke Hughes & Company furniture is designed for existing or historic buildings. Naturally enough, one of Luke's favourite subjects has generated a large number of pithy soundbites, many of which appear in company literature and promotional videos. 'You have to respond to the architecture,' he says. 'An understanding of architecture and the process of design, and sympathy for the architect who designed it, to me is key.'

Luke continues at greater length: 'Our attitude to architecture, old and new, is what distinguishes and differentiates us. It is the starting point for all of our activities. There has been one central idea behind Luke Hughes & Company's approach – that in any quality building, the connection between architecture and furniture should be seamless, creating a sense of "rightness", both functionally and aesthetically. Most buildings cannot function without the furniture, yet inappropriate furniture can grossly undermine great architecture.'

The additional subtlety of a furniture designer's relationship with historic architecture is made clear in a Luke Hughes & Company pamphlet describing what fine ecclesiastical buildings need, which increasingly points to flexibility and adaptability in what are now multi-functional spaces. Indeed, the same considerations apply to all historic buildings, whatever their function. The pamphlet reads: 'In our view, furniture should embellish the space, not embarrass it. This is particularly the case in Britain's major cathedrals, which offer the finest architectural interiors to be found anywhere in the world.

'But even historic interiors have to evolve if they are to remain relevant. This is due not only to changing social patterns and the reinterpretation of the liturgy but also to the development of new materials and the evolution of technology. It was always thus – the carpenter of the magnificent Octagon at Ely Cathedral [page 66] surely stood on the shoulders of the craftsmen descendants of those who built the great Norman transept at Winchester. For this reason, we continue to evolve our designs to reflect something of the spirit of this age as well as the intended architectural setting.

'The design criteria for cathedral furnishings demand more than mere aesthetic or practical considerations. Cathedrals serve broad communities – not only regular worshippers, but also county and civic dignitaries, the diocesan clergy team, local schools and colleges, and, more obviously, tourists. They all use the space for different reasons: for private prayer and reflection, for corporate worship, for meetings and conversation, for concerts and drama, for educational assemblies, or just a nice day out. There were 12 million visitors to UK cathedrals in 2016.

'So, when it comes to the furniture, the question is less about changing liturgy or about conservation of a heritage asset – it is about enabling a major community building (albeit one steeped in history, sentiment and splendour) to work, elegantly and efficiently. Much of this comes down to ergonomics and engineering.

'The key to a successful reordering is not only to respond to the architectural space and the way it is to be used but also to collaborate closely with the client to challenge and refine the brief, to develop something lasting well beyond what was initially envisaged. The design process depends on being able to work as a team and the most successful projects over the last thirty years or so are invariably those where the commissioners have a close working dialogue with the designers. Initial proposals are rarely the finished result and the best results are undoubtedly those where the

brief has been developed and refined, well beyond initial expectations.'

Luke's expressive comment on his own theme here relates to the briefing process mentioned earlier and gives a charming insight into his own response to buildings: he listens to them. 'The building is as much a client as the current occupier might be.'

The Luke Hughes 'statement of intent' continues with reflections on the variety of ages and styles in public architecture (mostly educational, institutional or liturgical), and the necessity of enabling its function: 'putting the building to work', as Luke calls it. 'The building types are as diverse as Norman Foster's School of Management for Yale University [page 180]; Michael Hopkins's Queen's Building at Emmanuel College, Cambridge [page 158]; or William the Conqueror's 11th-century Romanesque chapel in the Tower of London [page 87].

'One particular skill is to see beyond the immediate design brief of any project and predict how the furniture is likely to be used – not just for those who occupy these buildings but also for those whose job it is to manage them – without diminishing the dignity of the architecture.

'But furniture also has to work, and to last fifty years or more. So this is not just about aesthetics but also about engineering. We have evolved countless techniques for ensuring adaptability of the furniture – benches or chairs that stack, tables that fold, trolleys that make handling easier, felt pads to protect delicate architectural finishes [see Westminster Abbey's clergy furniture with adjustable feet, page 32].'

While the Luke Hughes approach to the architecture of historic interiors is well documented, it also pays us to consider the different set of client criteria generated by modern office buildings, represented here by the London offices of Diageo and Unilever (page 124). The story is of two table systems, originally conceived for different projects, but developed and installed with a keen consciousness of the need for flexibility in the era of cable management, and above all of installation cost. A change in the specification of the cabling, as seemed to happen almost annually in the 1980s and early 1990s before Wi-Fi became the norm, could cost as much as a complete new desk. 'With projects like this,' says Luke, 'the key to success is designing out some of the problems you get on site before you get to site. Having people on site is expensive, so you design for the absolute minimum of hassle.' Hence the development of a fully cable-managed table into a kit of parts assembled with a turnbuckle system that eliminated the need for any tools at all and radically reduced installation time on site. 'You're actually designing *process*. The installation and cable-management costs are about the same as the table itself. It's a "blind cost" that the client just has to meet willy-nilly. If we were clever with the design and used our brains, the client would save – but we needed to demonstrate that it is clever design.' From centuries-old godly piles to the fast-changing world of highly technologized knowledge work, 'clever design' as practised by Luke Hughes & Company always serves the building, and hence the multiple client groups. Only a deep love and understanding of architecture – and of people – can make design work this hard.

31 'Why did no one think of this before?' Stacking and moveable pews in Sheffield Cathedral. The trolleys are specially designed to balance the weight, which is carefully distributed in the design of the pews themselves.

32 The turnbuckle used in such office projects as those for Diageo and Unilever (page 124) to assemble furniture without tools. 'You are actually designing process, not just product,' says Luke.

Arts and Crafts and design

The persistent thread in the work of Luke Hughes is his lively and critical understanding of the Arts and Crafts tradition, and his own place as a furniture designer and maker within it. He is by no means a starry-eyed romantic, and since the formation of Luke Hughes & Company in the mid-1980s his concern has always been to engage with industry, to address production on an industrial scale, and to embrace the latest technology to that end. It has set up an equally lively and always healthy debate within and outside the company: every member of his team is passionately committed to its philosophy, and full of their own opinions – about the definition of craft, the value of the original Arts and Crafts ideals, and the complex relationship between craft and technology.

The key text in almost all Luke's thinking and writing about craft, as well as practising it, is a lecture he delivered to the Royal Society of Arts in 1999. In 2000 it was published in the *RSA Journal* and, in shortened form, *The Independent*, and has since appeared three times in updated form in *Crafts* magazine, the last in late 2017. Essentially, it is a kind of 'State of the Union' address for the crafts, dealing with their economic relevance as currently practised, the activity of the Crafts Council of Great Britain in respect of that relevance, and most importantly the attitudes and relationships of craftspeople to industry. It is worth noting that the 'Arts'

part of 'Arts and Crafts' does not play a significant part in Luke's analysis, short of referring occasionally to the decorative or applied arts. The original phrase comes from the formation of the Arts and Crafts Exhibition Society in 1887, when the terms had not reached a firm definition and were often interchangeable or taken to mean what we now think of as 'design'.

'My thesis is this,' says Luke. 'Modern artisans, building or craft, are as good as they have ever been. Only now they are better educated, work harder and are more financially acute than ever before. They have in their own workshops sophisticated industrial processes on a smaller, more economic scale than ever before. They understand the implications of technology and how to apply it, and, as a group of entrepreneurs, they have become an economic force of their own.'

The 2017 version of the lecture, as it appears in *Crafts* magazine, gives a vision of the future: 'After six frustrating years sitting on its board, I was much exercised about what the Crafts Council was for, how it could justify receiving public funds without proving economic relevance. I concluded: Who cares? The crafts should not just be about the occupation of the elderly in future years or even providing some spice to our aesthetic lives, some "pepper and salt" to our visual culture. It is also about employment and prosperity in a post-industrial world. There is a danger of thinking manufacturing has no place in our future. This is palpably nonsense. Industry has just become more

33 The Luke Hughes & Company team in July 2018 (see page 251 for a full list of names).

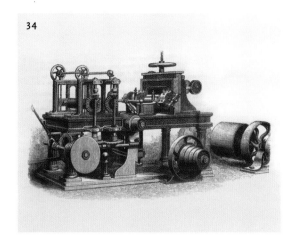

34 The Powis James planing machine, exhibited at the Great London Exposition of 1862. Such technology needed major capital investment, in contrast to today's accessibly priced digitally controlled equipment.

35 Assembling the 'devilishly difficult' top rail of the re-engineered Coventry chair. Even in highly technologized processes, skilled craftsmanship abides.

36 Gordon Russell, the link between Arts and Crafts and modern industrial design and production. Unlike Luke Hughes, Russell was not a craftsman himself, but he was immensely influential in bringing the message of good design to consumers.

complex. With emerging industries in the Far East, it is clear we cannot compete on price so there is only one option, to add value through quality. For that we clearly need the craftsman-designers, we need the small producers and we need them to be able to find each other.'

Production and labour

As Arts and Crafts pioneers, John Ruskin and William Morris concerned themselves with labour as found in the factories of mass production. In the 21st century Arts and Crafts tradition, as practised by Luke Hughes & Company, mass production is unknown. All the labour that the company engages with is highly skilled; they are craftspeople, in other words. It is actually technology that throws a new light on this distinction, because before small workshops had the ability to produce wooden items in large quantities to engineering tolerances – such as the 1,500 Coventry chairs for Valparaiso University Chapel – all they could aspire to was 'batch production', which is counted in the 10s, 20s and 30s. Now there is such a thing as 'mass batch' production. But it still does not engage the disempowered worker in the faceless factory, who may or may not find solace in art, as Morris believed. With one or two notable exceptions, Luke Hughes does not

manufacture for private clients – all the company's current production is for public places – and he does not manufacture in automated factories using unskilled labour.

Design

Luke's journey as a craftsman-maker, through a (short) phase of being a designer-maker, then an even shorter one as manufacturer, has led him to his current occupation as a designer. Because of his making background and his classically 'overeducated' intellect, he is a most unusual specimen of the breed. He engages with not only the production process but also the myriad of economic and social ramifications of creating furniture that serves its architectural context and its clients' functional and economic needs, while considering the science of materials and their sustainability and, above all, how people use space. This is why he calls himself a 'social anthropologist'.

Gordon Russell, born in 1892 and arguably the most successful 'bridge' between the ideals of the Victorian Arts and Crafts movement and the imperatives of 20th-century design and production, is key to understanding how Luke Hughes has developed his own relationship to the Arts and Crafts tradition in an emphatically modern and technological context. In his

37 The Assembly chair produced for Corpus Christi College, Cambridge, in 1991. The modelling created by subtle decorative detail picks up light and shade in the linenfold panelling. The 'rhythm of quantity' can be clearly seen in fig. 26.

much-celebrated lecture 'Skill', delivered to the Faculty of the Royal Designers for Industry at the Royal Society of Arts in 1978, near the end of his life, Russell – who described himself as a 'designer of furniture' in his military Officer's Record Book as early as 1917 – recalled: 'I saw that the Arts and Crafts leaders were trying to bring designer and maker together, in itself a most worthy objective, but by insisting that the craftsman should design everything that he made they went a bit too far ... it became clear that the designer must have a thorough knowledge of methods of production, whether by hand or machine.'

The link between Luke Hughes & Company and Gordon Russell Ltd is a direct one, of course, in the person of someone we have met already – Ray Leigh, formerly design director then managing director of Gordon Russell Ltd, and chairman and non-executive director of Luke Hughes & Company. Luke is often heard to repeat with relish Gordon Russell's pithy mantra, drawn from Russell's autobiography, *Designer's Trade*: 'The most urgent job of all was to teach the machine manners.' The clear bloodline of design descent from Russell to Hughes is most eloquently expressed in the Coventry Cathedral chair, the original version of which was designed by Dick Russell for Basil Spence's magnificent celebration of the new, postwar,

reconstructed Britain, as well as a memorial to the old. The Luke Hughes version for Valparaiso University Chapel, Indiana, is at once a homage and a sensitive but comprehensive redesign, where the increased section of almost every component, and the techniques by which the complex curved and rebated back rail is machined, show a true engineering strand in the company's design DNA. Luke's production director, Nigel Shepherd, and his design manager, Stephen Sharp, are both full of respect, as much for the aesthetics as for the production design of the chair, whose legs are joined to the box frame in a satisfyingly ingenious, strong and yet very simple joint.

A single specific example gives a clear insight into the maturity and intellectual depth of Luke Hughes's design process, in this case the 'quirk and chamfer' details, small mouldings on the edges of certain chair components. The chairs for Corpus Christi dining hall were the first Luke ever made – 'I was a bit nervous' – but he explains how the play of light and shadow in the hall's linenfold panelling has been picked up in the modelling of the chair itself: 'There is a lot of light and shade. This modelling is especially effective when you see them in quantity. One chair looks like a chair, but when you see 100 or 500 or 1,500 in a room, the effect is completely different. We have to consider the rhythm of quantity.'

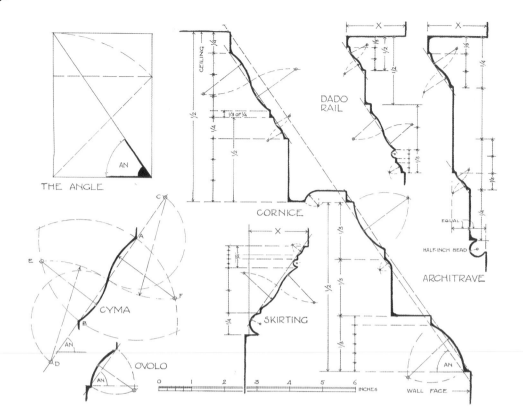

THE ANGLE

CYMA

OVOLO

CEILING

CORNICE

SKIRTING

DADO RAIL

ARCHITRAVE

HALF-INCH BEAD

EQUAL

WALL FACE

0 1 2 3 4 5 6 INCHES

38 Living by the golden section: sketches from the hand of Sir Edwin Lutyens showing how he derived the angles, curves and cornice details for many of his architectural commissions. Thanks are due to Sir Edwin's son, Robert, for the gift of the original to Luke's mother.

On the wall of one of the meeting rooms at the Luke Hughes & Company studio is a print of a detail sketch from the hand of none other than Sir Edwin Lutyens. 'The moulding detail is constructed according to a set of rules,' says Luke. 'It goes back to Alberti, the Renaissance architect who took inspiration from Vitruvius. The angles in which the mouldings work are related to angles of the sun and the way the shadows fall. You have a box cornice and a skirting detail, both created in the golden section, and the quirk detail gives a softer edge and a depth of shadow.

'Because of my making background I understand how to achieve that modelling and its effect. A 2-millimetre router bit, for example, will create the stopped chamfer that was common in the 15th century. A lot of success in our major projects has been based on the judicious use of shadow gaps, which conceal the visual effect of timber shrinkage and expansion. An architect like Alan Stanton, for instance [of Stanton Williams, architects of the Sainsbury Laboratory at Cambridge University, page 203], implicitly understands shadow gaps. It's the sort of thing that makes working with him such a joy.'

Materials and sustainability

Materials are one of Luke's passions, and the use and abuse of them have a number of connections to the overriding company philosophy. His unpretentious but rigorous intellect flexes its muscles on the subjects of shrinkage and expansion of timber according to moisture content, the 'modulus of rupture' (how easily it splits), specific gravity and a host of other mechanical properties; the liturgical furniture in Westminster Abbey, for instance, is made in walnut, which has almost half the specific gravity of oak, as a move both to preserve the delicate Cosmati pavement, and to make it easier for the vergers to move. He also believes that a relationship with materials is one of the principles of the Arts and Crafts movement: 'Knowing the craft of building, that's what Arts and Crafts is about. Knowing your materials and how to use them. If you don't know what the properties of the materials you're using are, how you work them, then how can you possibly know what they can do for you? I'm always appalled by how little time in design colleges is spent on this.'

Luke has done his bit to counteract this general ignorance, teaching a module on timber on the architecture degree course at the University of Cambridge at the behest of one of his favourite modern

39 The secret of the turning moment and why chair legs split: a page from the 1990s report of the Cambridge University engineering department on studies into the relative strength and durability of timbers and adhesives used for chairs.

The Problem of Turning Moments

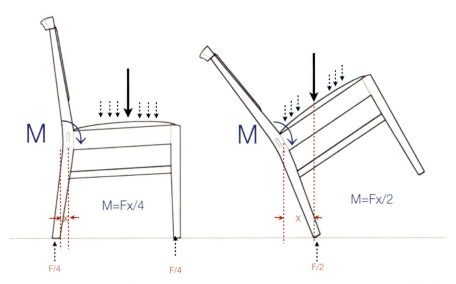

Fig 2a. Least severe case of loading   Fig 2b. Worst case of loading

architects, Eric Parry, whose practice occupied the upper floors of his Covent Garden workshop in the early days. He also engaged the services of W. Phillip Beattie, of the Cambridge University engineering department, in the late 1990s, working closely with him to establish what went wrong in a batch of chairs that failed to an unacceptable degree in an overheated merchant bank. The results of the testing and research identified weaknesses in the jointing, unexpected problems in the kind of glue used, and the excessively dry atmosphere. This kind of scientific approach is yet another factor that sets Luke Hughes and his company apart; no other furniture maker of his generation, large factory or small workshop, engages with engineering expertise to such a degree. 'It's all very well to have a feel for what walnut, for instance, will do, but can you measure how easily it will split? Yes, you can, but you need an engineer to help you. It's not just touchy-feely; you need maths. You can apply the maths without killing the spontaneity.'

Sustainability, of course, is an issue right at the heart of a company whose raw material is mostly timber. Typically, Luke Hughes combines common sense with disciplined adherence to sustainability guidelines and assurances that the timber used comes with appropriate provenance and reliable benchmarking. But it is also a matter of longevity: the Luke Hughes

brand document created in 2013 devotes a whole section to the company's environmental statement: 'Our business was founded on principles of environmental responsibility. The longer a building and its furniture stay relevant, the longer the carbon stays locked up. The longer it stays locked up, the less we contribute to CO_2 emissions. Long life equates to locked-up carbon. We design for long life, thirty to fifty years minimum.

'Sixty-five per cent of the materials we use are timber. There are few more environmentally sound materials than timber, assuming forest extraction schemes are respected and not abused.

'Sustainably managed forests convert CO_2 into oxygen as trees grow but also remove and store carbon within the timber. This is then used to make our furniture that becomes a carbon sink for the long life of the furniture.

'We have a strict company policy to buy solid hardwoods from suppliers who derive their raw material from forests managed to the standards of FSC, PEFC, SFI or equivalent, where replanting and controlled felling are part of the overall plan.

'We actively support tree-planting schemes and are founder members of Woodland Heritage Trust. We do not use any timbers listed as endangered through the

40 Restoring the priceless Cosmati pavement in Westminster Abbey in 2009. Walnut was chosen for the liturgical furniture because of its low specific gravity.

CITES [Convention on International Trade in Endangered Species of Wild Fauna and Flora]. The particle boards and veneers that we use come from forests in Western and Central Europe, USA and Canada and are 99 per cent recyclable by weight.

'All of our production meets E1 standard (EN13986) of ultra-flow formaldehyde emissions. Glue used to attach edges on tables is water-based and releases no VOCs [volatile organic compounds].

'All steel products are manufactured from 100 per cent recycled scrap and are themselves 100 per cent recyclable.' Enough said.

Craft, cognitive process and a technologized future

For a final assessment of the place of Luke Hughes and his eponymous company in the English furniture tradition generally, and the Arts and Crafts version specifically, it is useful to refer to the work of Matthew Crawford, an American political philosopher and motorcycle restorer, whose project has been to explore the flawed process by which manual work has always been assigned lower social and professional status than knowledge work. Crawford's book *Shopcraft as Soulcraft: An Inquiry into the Value of Work* (2009), the UK edition of which is entitled *The Case for Working With Your Hands, or Why Office Work Is Bad for Us and Fixing*

Things Feels Good, could have been written for Luke Hughes, one of whose most passionate beliefs is the Arts and Crafts maxim of Lawrence Pearsall Jacks, an author and educationalist from the early 20th century: 'Every rise in the quality of the work which a man does is followed swiftly and inevitably by a rise in the quality of the man who does it,' he says (taken from *Responsibility and Culture*, a collection of lectures published by Yale University Press in 1924).

'The degradation of work is ultimately a cognitive matter, rooted in the separation of thinking from doing,' adds Crawford. 'I often find manual work more engaging intellectually ... My purpose ... is to elaborate the potential for human flourishing in the manual trades – their rich cognitive challenges and psychic nourishment.'

Which, to repeat Luke's phrase, is where we came in: 'There's something incredibly important about working with your hands.' With this recognition – that manual work is just as inherently intellectually valuable as knowledge work – comes a radical reassessment of the social attitudes still inherent in education, production and consumerism; and much of it is dependent on our relationship to tools. As robots and 'deep learning' machines snap at our cognitive heels, I will take the liberty of quoting from my own book *The Ecology of*

41 Luke Hughes & Company production director Nigel Shepherd (second from left) during the timber selection process for the Valparaiso Chapel of Resurrection chairs.

42 Trevor Ballinger (left) and Alan Harvey of Fine Furniture Designs, the Cotswold workshop that has made more than 7 million pounds' worth of Luke Hughes furniture since 1990. Both men formerly worked for Gordon Russell Ltd, based just a few miles from their current site.

43 Steve Jones (left) and Kevin Adams, of the Shrewsbury-based bespoke joinery firm Davies Shaw, during work on the Keystone Academy project (page 222).

44 Richard Mouland, one of the original Luke Hughes & Company making team at the Tisbury facility in 1990, holding a table-top lectern for St John's College, Cambridge, made in his own workshop near Salisbury.

the Soul (2016), which is a kind of meditation manual, coming at the notion of craftsmanship from the emotional, even spiritual, realm of which Luke speaks in his letters quoted earlier: 'Craftsmanship ... is another way of saying "mindfulness". When I give lectures on design and craft to design students, I start with this proposition to get them thinking: "Design is an activity. Craft is a state of mind." There's nothing in life ... to which you can't apply a principle of craftsmanship. There's nothing you do ... that can't be done better if you approach it with total attention, total commitment, total absorption. Love, in other words. All these things go to make up craftsmanship, a craftsman-like attitude to the task at hand, a devotion to that task for its own beautiful sake. No accomplished craftsperson will deny that the key ingredient is love. You apply love, approach the task with it; and then the task itself, and the end result, show it back to you and to others who enjoy it.'

And that is why the true spirit of the Arts and Crafts tradition – or perhaps we should say just the craft tradition – abides in the people, the work and the heavily technologized design and production systems of Luke Hughes & Company. And it is why the robots will never win; they will never love their work.

PLACES OF
WORSHIP

Twenty-four cathedrals, more than a hundred parish churches, a generous handful of synagogues – and counting. Luke Hughes furniture is now almost ubiquitous in the estate of the Church of England (and of Scotland), not to mention New York's best-known progressive synagogue (page 98) and the astonishing, 2,000-seat Chapel of the Resurrection at Valparaiso University, Indiana (page 106), for which Luke Hughes & Company redesigned and re-engineered the quintessentially 'British Modernist' Coventry chair.

The projects in this section vary enormously. The comprehensive reworking of the crossing under Ely Cathedral's breathtaking Octagon (page 66 and opposite) included an entirely new altar on a moveable dais, altar rails, clergy furniture and choir stalls, conductor's stand, credence table and more; at the other end of the scale is the small but perfectly formed sixteen-seat Venerable Chapel in Winchester Cathedral (page 52), the centrepiece of which is a new stone altar with a luminous panel of perforated aluminium by the artist Rachel Schwalm.

We begin, however, with Westminster Abbey, largely because it is one of the world's best-known places of worship, and not least because tens of millions of people watched the wedding of Prince William and Kate Middleton on television, making the Luke Hughes sacristy furniture the most televised furniture in the world. The engineering solution to the problem of

preserving the recently restored 13th-century decorative Cosmati pavement, whose irregularities amounted to several centimetres, demonstrates the studio's approach to problem-solving: 'thinking outside of the box' – what used to be called 'lateral thinking' – is apparent everywhere in the work.

We group together the cathedrals of Bristol (page 44), Winchester, Sheffield (page 58) and Ely, but St Giles's in Edinburgh stands on its own. The monolithic marble block that makes up the whole project is a work apart, although the preliminary – what might be called the 'pre-design' process – is much the same, based on painstaking research and Luke's own sense of the 'numinous', that mixture of gravity and lightness that comes with a truly spiritual interior.

Innovative thinking is a theme that links all the projects in this book, but in the case of places of worship, the stacking pew is definitely one of those 'why did no one think of this before?' pieces. Best illustrated in the Sheffield Cathedral story, it also emphasizes the Luke Hughes approach to making a building more efficient and more enjoyable to be in simply by making the right furniture. Luke calls it 'putting the building to work', and we see that stream of design thinking throughout these pages.

SACRARIUM CLERGY FURNITURE, WESTMINSTER ABBEY

A priceless pavement and a marvel of engineering

'We have done several projects for Westminster Abbey,' says Luke, counting off on his fingers the Cellarium café in one of the oldest parts of the building; the furniture in the Pyx Chamber, where gold and silver coins kept in 'pyxes', or wooden boxes, were trialled for purity; and the Song School for the abbey's choir. 'But the most entertaining project was the sanctuary furniture for the Sacrarium – more or less the most sacred part of the abbey, where the Coronation Chair is situated.'

Westminster – which, perversely, is technically neither a cathedral nor an abbey, but a 'Royal Peculiar' directly responsible to the sovereign, with no bishops between the dean and chapter and royalty itself – started life in the 10th century as a Benedictine monastery. It was greatly enlarged as St Peter's Abbey by Edward the Confessor in the mid-11th century, and transformed again in the French Gothic style by Henry III between 1245 and 1260. Henry, determined to establish his line's claim to the throne, wanted a holy place of worship that would also house the consecration and burial of monarchs. As part of this reinvention, he commissioned the Cosmati pavement, a glorious and intricate mosaic, for the floor in front of the High Altar.

The pavement takes its name from the Cosmati family of craftsmen who originated this type of inlaid-stone decoration, using a variety of semi-precious stones including onyx, porphyry, green serpentine and yellow limestone. The Roman Cosmati specialist Odoricus and his team of imported craftsmen completed the pavement in 1268, the finest surviving example of Cosmati work north of the Alps. Since the 1870s, however, it had been obscured by thick carpets, as well as having suffered the ravages of time.

Aware that a royal wedding was in the offing, and that, logically, another coronation would not be that long in coming, the dean and chapter commissioned the uncovering and restoration of the pavement in 2010. As part of that project they also commissioned Luke Hughes

BELOW The West Towers were completed in 1745 to a design by Nicholas Hawksmoor. Rising to more than 30 metres (100 ft), the breathtaking Gothic vaulted ceiling is the highest in England.

OPPOSITE Built, or assembled, over a five-hundred-year period – and with work still going on – Westminster Abbey has a more direct connection to the historic heart of England than any other single building. Most of the main fabric dates from Henry III's time, 1245 to 1268, including the Cosmati pavement, an extraordinarily intricate masterpiece of devotional craftsmanship in the Sacrarium, the space reserved for coronations, just east of the crossing. The Luke Hughes & Company liturgical furniture can be seen to the left and right of the altar.

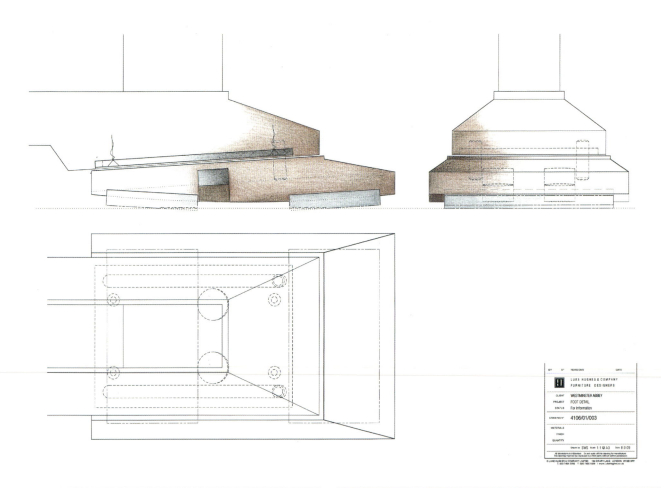

OPPOSITE, TOP Drawing detail of the magnetic sliding-wedge system that allows the chairs and benches to be levelled easily, on a surface that varies in height by up to 40 millimetres (1⁵/₈ in.). The felt pads also protect the priceless pavement.

OPPOSITE, BOTTOM Aspect views of a liturgical clergy chair. The curve of the arm is a reference to Charlemagne's throne at Aachen, a form used in other Luke Hughes & Company furniture – for example, the Wykeham chairs in Bristol Cathedral's music library (page 47). The scalloped seat pan gives greater comfort during those lengthy sermons.

RIGHT Direct side elevation of one of the benches, with exactly the same arm detail at either end and a clear view of the wedges at work. The central arms join the frame below the top rail, which is why they are visible through the end opening.

& Company to design and make new clergy furniture, because, says Luke, 'the old Victorian oak furniture – which was probably designed by George Gilbert Scott – was likely to damage or dislodge the newly-set semi-precious stones. It was heavy and difficult to move.

'The main problem was that the floor had been subject to so much wear and tear that it was incredibly uneven, with variations of up to 40 millimetres (1⁵/₈ in.). Our brief was to come up with something light that could accommodate all the clergy who might be involved in major ceremonial roles – not only state occasions but also the liturgy of weekly worship – but it had to more or less disappear. Not only should it not call attention to itself, it also had to self-level to protect the floor, and also solve instability issues on such an uneven surface.

'So we designed a system of sliding wedges. Felt pieces are deeply inset into the floor face of the wedge, which is also slightly curved. The actual foot has a steel plate embedded in it, with industrial magnets to hold the wedge wherever it stops. The vergers can pick up a four-seater and fix any discrepancy by simply kicking the wedges in or out.

'We made the benches and chairs in walnut, which has 65 per cent of the specific gravity of oak, almost half the weight. Suddenly the furniture was playing a part in supporting the liturgy, which was part of my thinking all along – what it would look like when "dressed" with clergy in their rich vestments, and what it would look like when it was empty. The need to disappear was key.

'The first state occasion for the new furniture was not actually a moment of state, but the visit of His Holiness Pope Benedict XVI in 2010. The big state event was the royal wedding of William and Kate in 2011, watched by an estimated 162 million people worldwide, when you could argue that our work became the most televised furniture in the world.'

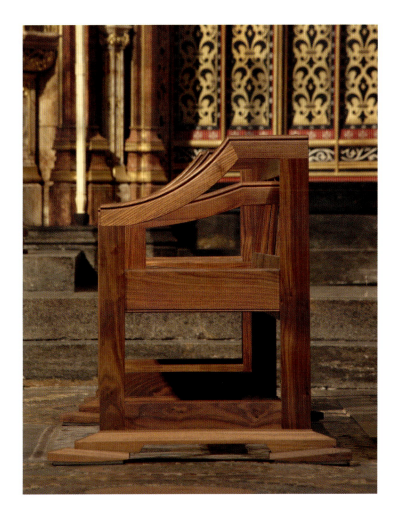

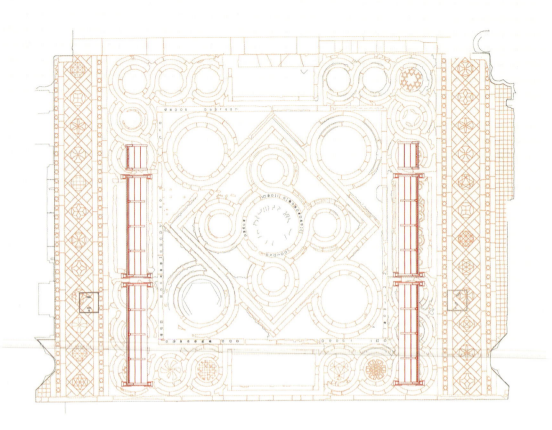

PREVIOUS PAGES Bench and chair posed in front of the High Altar.

LEFT AND OPPOSITE, TOP Schematic drawing of the Cosmati pavement with the location of the chairs and benches marked. The image on the facing page shows how the intricate pattern of the floor's geometric design looks today. It is symmetrical in layout but not in infill: the variations are endless. No two roundels are the same; of the four 'orbiting' roundels, one is circular, one hexagonal, one heptagonal and one octagonal. It is built up from pieces of stone of different colours and sizes cut into a variety of shapes: triangles, squares, circles, rectangles and many others. The central roundel is made of onyx, while the pavement also includes purple porphyry, green serpentine and yellow limestone. In a departure from standard Italian practice, pieces of opaque coloured glass – red, turquoise, cobalt blue and bluish white – are also used.

LEFT, BOTTOM, AND OPPOSITE, BOTTOM Schematic dimensioned drawing of the four-seater bench, with another view on the facing page.

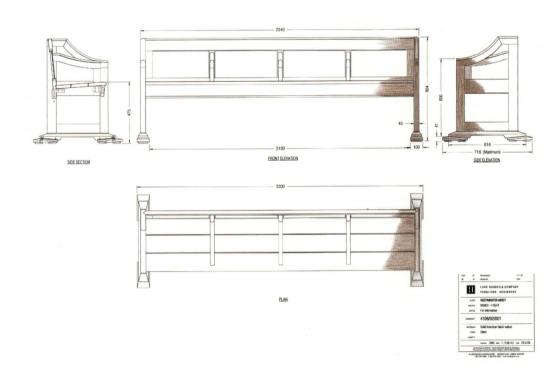

There is usually a moment of light relief in such stories, especially when dealing with a solemn coterie of elevated clerics such as the dean and chapter of Westminster Abbey. 'I took some samples of very powerful industrial magnets into a meeting with the dean and chapter,' says Luke, 'to explain my idea and how the wedges would work. Perhaps unsurprisingly, the floor was uneven, so one of them rolled off the table and into the dean's lap. All was well, or so we thought, until I got a call later that day to say that the magnet had comprehensively wiped all the data off the dean's mobile phone. Emails, pictures, contacts, diary – everything. What could I say? I hoped he had backed it up!'

BELOW The Royal Wedding of HRH Prince William, Duke of Cambridge, and Catherine Middleton in Westminster Abbey on 29 April 2011. A million people lined the route between the abbey and Buckingham Palace; 37 million people watched it on television in the UK, and there were 72 million live streams on YouTube worldwide. Luke Hughes's claim that his furniture became the most televised in the world is hard to deny.

OPPOSITE American black walnut and multicoloured patterned inlay go together. The driver for the choice of timber, apart from its smooth, rich appearance, was the need to minimize weight, which could damage the newly restored floor. Walnut has 65 per cent of the specific gravity of oak – nearly half the weight.

FOUR CATHEDRALS

One Octagon, three altars, and mobile pews and choir stalls for the modern world

The four cathedrals in this section are presented together because, although in each case the architecture and the functional brief are specific to the building, Luke Hughes & Company's response – the principle underlying the design stages – is always to make the building work better. Luke uses such phrases as 'enable the architecture', 'management of the building' and 'the whole industry of what goes on in a huge, busy building like a cathedral', turning the attention as much to process and efficiency as to aesthetics. 'If you get the furniture right,' he says, 'you are doing more than just designing pretty pieces. It helps the whole process. Every fifteen minutes you can take off the management of all these disparate elements – things, people, activities – makes a huge difference.'

In the case of Bristol Cathedral (page 44), for which the company undertook four separate projects between 2000 and 2002, the 'key principle' for the Song School and music library, says Luke, 'was to enable the director of music to manage the music more efficiently by getting the shelving and storage right.' Similarly, the mobile choir stalls that can be moved between the Lady Chapel and the nave enable the vergers to meet the shifting demands on the space and make it work more efficiently.

At Ely (page 66), nearly twenty years later, Luke is enthusiastic about using engineering techniques in wood and steel to design and make the new moveable altar and choir furniture. 'The theme is enabling the variety of functions to happen. It all revolves around the architecture and how you inhabit that space. That's what we do. We start with the function, so the space planning, the massing and the proportions are all key. If you don't get this right, you might as well not start.'

Functional requirements combine with innovative design thinking – often spurred by tight budgets – to initiate new product types capable of serving the changing needs of ancient buildings striving to respond to new social patterns and behaviours. Until after the Reformation of the 16th century, congregations stood for services. Later, the preaching of the Word become more important than the celebration of the Eucharist, and the provision of pews became the norm. However, their fixed positions greatly restricted the use of what had once been open space. Luke Hughes & Company pioneered the concept of stacking pews, a beautifully simple answer to the modern need for churches to clear the floor for yoga classes, nursery schools and other such activities. Choir stalls on wheels, and even a moveable altar, are part of the same phenomenon.

In Sheffield (page 58), the Luke Hughes & Company stacking bench – not a pew – comes into its own. 'If you don't understand the architecture and those who inhabit it, all you're doing is making product,' says Luke. 'We're not. We are coming up with genuine ways to make people's lives better, to give them greater comfort and a greater sense of purpose, to enjoy these extraordinary spaces. I don't think about how to sell product. I'm always thinking about how to make the building work better.'

Winchester's Venerable Chapel (page 52), in a class of its own for size and spirituality, is a gem. The exploration by both designer and artist of the bare function of devotional furniture illuminates that very function, which we feel as a beautiful and uplifting presence, creating unearthly light in a tiny space (the chapel holds sixteen people). Not what you'd call a cathedral at all, but one of those hidden delights of English religious buildings, a miniature of charm and refuge.

At the beginning of this century, the time of the company's first cathedral commission in Bristol, Luke attended numerous conferences about liturgical furniture. 'Talking to the dean and canons, I really learnt the problems of managing the building. It's not just because I studied medieval history at Cambridge University. I was at the choir school of Salisbury Cathedral myself; I practically lived in the cathedral when I was growing up. I already knew the language, and I also knew how the Salisbury Song School was laid out. It never worked very well. Listening to the vergers and understanding the problems of moving stuff around has ended up informing every cathedral job we've done.'

OPPOSITE Clockwise from top left: Ely has two towers, the one seen here housing the Octagon, one of the most magnificent pieces of ecclesiastical architecture in the UK, if not Europe. The other, higher tower at the west end can just be seen. Bristol, whose 14th-century choir 'proves ... that English design surpasses that of all other countries', according to Nikolaus Pevsner; Sheffield, the quintessential urban cathedral, whose ministry to the town is very much alive; and Winchester, where the tiny Venerable Chapel was made to glow with unearthly light from Rachel Schwalm's illuminated altar artwork.

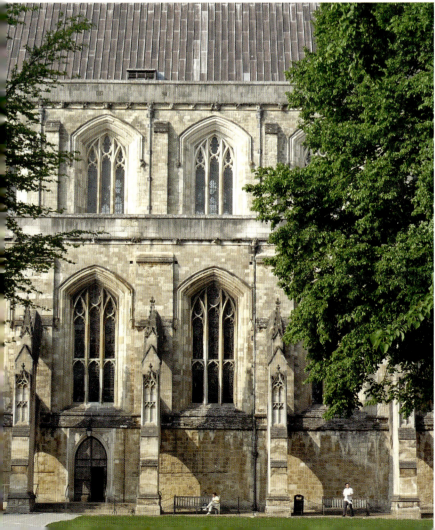
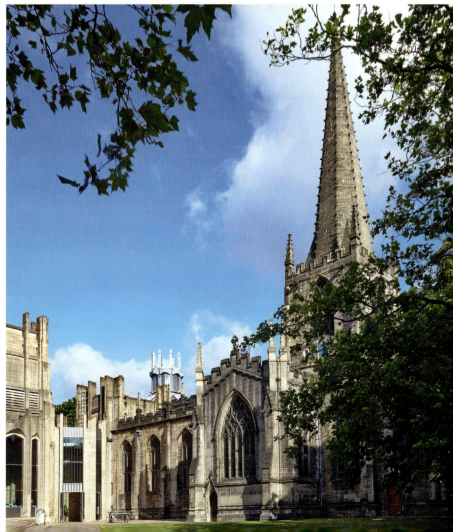

BRISTOL CATHEDRAL

Four stories of rationalization and mobility

Bristol Cathedral, founded in 1140 as St Augustine's Abbey, has been an architectural work in progress for almost nine hundred years. Additions, demolitions and rebuildings were concentrated in the 12th, 13th and 14th to 16th centuries, with much of the recognizable decorative Gothic fabric taking shape in the late 14th and early 15th. Significant changes in both the sprawling collection of buildings and their official position in the changing diocesan landscape coincided with Henry VIII's dissolution of the monasteries in the mid-16th century, part of his radical and revolutionary creation of the Church of England.

When the Gothic Revival took hold in Britain in the mid-19th century, G. E. Street, architect of the Royal Courts of Justice in London, designed in the 1870s a new nave based on original 15th-century plans. A few years later, John Loughborough Pearson's west front with its twin towers was completed in 1888.

The building boasts no less than three unique vaults, and some of the first uses of pointed arches in Britain.

The architectural historian Nikolaus Pevsner wrote of the early 14th-century choir of Bristol that, 'from the point of view of spatial imagination', it is not only superior to anything else in England or Europe but 'proves incontrovertibly that English design surpasses that of all other countries' at that date (*The Buildings of England: North Somerset and Bristol*, 1958).

The first cathedral job for Luke Hughes, Bristol has a special place in the collective heart of the company. It eventually turned into four separate projects: the music library; the Song School; flexible and mobile choir stalls for the nave; and a new supplementary altar and plinth that could be installed in the nave, forward of the choir, and easily stowed in the Newton Chapel.

The original call came in 1997 from the director of music, Mark Lee, who had been an organ scholar at Corpus Christi College, Cambridge, when a youthful Luke had taken on the furnishing of the college's choir library. The first meeting was in 1999, focused on the poky and inconvenient corridor, not much bigger than an

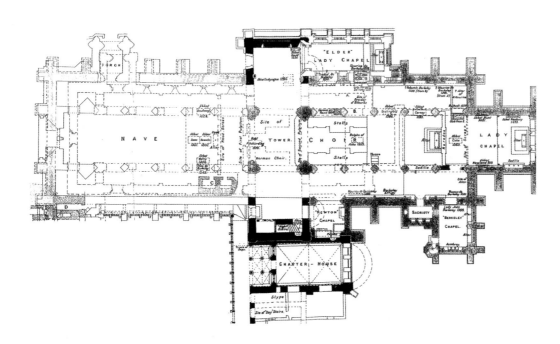

old-fashioned railway carriage, where the twenty-four-part scores of the cathedral's vast music collection were about to be moved. It was not an encouraging sight.

'What we ended up doing,' says Luke, 'was creating this rather Soane-ian space to make the most of the railway-carriage proportions. The biggest functional problem we had to solve was music management, rather than the storage itself; if you have twenty-four parts, you need a place to lay out and organize the scores and put them back quickly. Every minute of time you can save for someone who does that daily can go into the other richnesses of the place – such as the music. That's "management of the building".

'There was a lot of discussion about how to pull the printed music out, give it a sorting tray, read it and tuck it back in. Then what about access to the upper shelves, when the sorting trays are out? Things like that.'

The solutions, as you might expect, are both functionally and visually elegant. The rich warmth of the light oak that now forms the newly vaulted ceiling helps to define the space; but with its inset lighting, it achieves the effect of much greater height, making a coherence of line, colour and form with the sliding panelled doors, which reach floor to ceiling and add their own vertical emphasis to the space. The red wall

paint and restored and refinished parquet flooring further warm and lighten the surfaces. Pull-out sorting trays line the cupboards at desk height, hiding behind the sliding doors until they are needed, and the gently curved and tapered sides of the library steps, together with the sweeping arms of the Bradfield chair, offer mild relief to all the linearity. It is a pleasant space to inhabit and work, and functionally as neat and efficient as you could hope for.

Mark and his colleagues, says Luke, had got the bit between their teeth. 'They said, "Let's replace the old music desks in the Song School, which don't work. We want something where the boys can tuck the benches in, stand up and move around, move the desks themselves, maybe perch on them – so we can rearrange the room as often as we like."' The old desks are captured in a photographic-print 'triptych' created by Luke and his team – a pre-digital method of depicting a large space during a project's planning stages.

The result was the light music stand-cum-storage shelving in quartered European oak on small-diameter steel uprights, with matching benches that would sit within the vertical volume of the piece so the boys could sit or stand by choice. The angled top surfaces for holding the scores, with their heavily chamfered edges

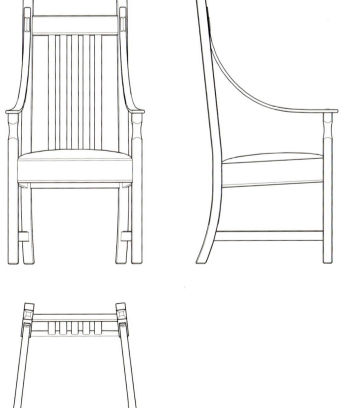

and large central cut-outs, create an atmosphere of lightness and flexibility, as well as delivering in practical terms. It is a common theme in Luke Hughes & Company pieces to maximize the passage of natural light through an interior by using a frame instead of a solid surface, or removing material from it.

'"Great", said the music department,' recalls Luke. '"You've transformed our lives. Now can you come and have a look at the choir area?"' Most of the services during the week were in the Lady Chapel, but the department wanted to be able to move the choir into the nave for the much bigger Eucharist service on Sunday, or even have the choir in the actual choir space of the cathedral for evensong, for example. It called for another set of lightweight and even more mobile choir stalls that would be easy to move from the Lady Chapel into the body of the church itself, forward of the rood screen and close to the congregation. The solution was a variant of the lightweight stalls in the Song School but this time in oak, while the metal frames were actually mounted on castors. The powder coating on the steel is a lighter and rather more reserved shade of grey, and the open panels in the Song School version are here given a more formal infill. Charterhouse stacking benches are used instead of the rectilinear and strictly functional seating of the Song School.

The *pièce de résistance*, however, was the mobile altar. It was as if the cathedral's precentor, Brendan Clover, and his colleagues had been saving the best till last. As well as a more mobile choir, now able to engage with the congregation in the body of the church, 'they needed an altar that they could bring forward of the choir into the nave,' says Luke. 'It had to work without conflicting with the presence of the high altar, which can be seen through the length of the building.' That went without question, but the sense of inclusion of the congregation, the breaking of the bread and performance of the sacrament right in the 'public' area of the church, was vitally important to the change in the liturgy suggested during the Second Vatican Council of 1962–65. Pope John XXIII's initiative was to 'open the windows of the Church and let in some fresh air'; and although the Church of England does not take direct orders from the Pope, the newer ecumenical spirit prevails. Thus, to bring the Eucharist into the body of the congregation, another altar was needed.

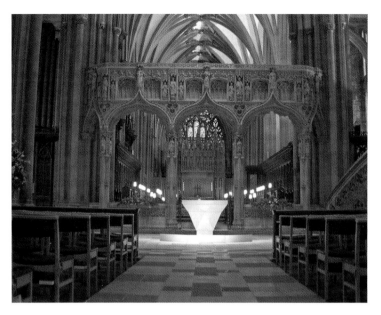

ABOVE Two views of the flat, MDF mock-ups for the new altar, used to test proportions and massing. Directional lighting and the plinth help preserve the sense of sacredness in the secular space; the altar's weight and dimensions were critical, as it had to be moved up and down steps by two people and stored with the choir stalls in the Newton Chapel.

But it had to be moveable by no more than two people, it had to go up and down two steps on its way to and from the Newton Chapel in the south transept, opposite the 'Elder' Lady Chapel in the north, and it had to be no more than 1,340 millimetres (52¾ in.) wide so it would go through the opening in the medieval screen leading to the Newton Chapel. A plinth was also needed, and since the altar was to inhabit the 'secular' nave, as opposed to the 'sacred' choir space, it needed to have as much dignity and gravitas as possible. 'The plinth gives the altar a sense of the sacred,' says Luke, 'but we also decided to give the plinth a flooring pattern to reflect the floor in the choir – to add to the sense of "otherness". We used the octagon principle, which creates shadows and extra modelling by the rhythm of shading you get from the shapes. The whole point of the flooring pattern is that it throws light back. And looking down on the top, you can see the four crosses we made by playing with the octagon shapes. An altar is supposed to have five crosses, but there is the central cross on top as well. We managed to incorporate the symbolism in quite an abstract, geometric way.' In a silent salute to the Arts and Crafts tradition, the gold-leaf carved lettering was designed by Richard Kindersley and executed by Philip Surey. Images of the

new nave altar, past which the high altar can be seen in the distance, attest to the success of the hierarchy and of the second altar's grace and presence.

High Church or Low? The Church of England does not respond directly to edicts from the Holy See, but the story is given a wry twist in the tail by the obvious High Church inclinations of the cathedral's precentor. 'The Protestant Church discourages the keeping of relics,' says Luke. 'It was one of the tenets of Luther's Reformation. But Brendan took me aside out of hearing of his colleagues, held up a 35mm film-roll canister, and asked, "Do you think you could find room for this in the new altar?" "What is it?" I asked. "St Jerome's fingernail," came the reply. Well, whatever I may think about that, I can tell you he is in there. He isn't accessible, but he's there.'

RIGHT The altar's five-cross symbolism using the geometrical pattern of crossing veneers is visible when the altar is viewed directly from above; the fifth cross is the large one formed by the parallel lines. The octagonal shape and cross-matched chequerboard-laid veneers reflect the floor pattern of the choir – a sacred space – and carry it into the secular nave, where the reflected light adds to the sense of 'otherness'.

BELOW The angular jointing of the veneered panels, offset by gilded seams or contrasting timbers, ensures a constant play of light and shade. The gilded lettering of the text in Latin ('Jesus Christ is the same yesterday and today and for ever'; Hebrews 13:8) was designed by Richard Kindersley and cut by Philip Surey.

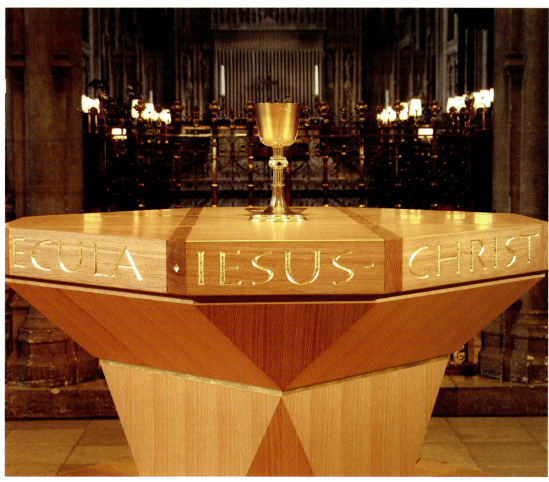

VENERABLE CHAPEL, WINCHESTER CATHEDRAL

Small, perfectly formed and numinous

'It was a lovely job,' says Luke, poring over the plan of the sixteen-seat Venerable Chapel in Winchester Cathedral's south transept. 'A tiny little side chapel, and it was our job to come up with something to make this space for early morning prayer really spiritual.' Existing furniture, which consisted of early Victorian prayer desks spectacularly ill-matched to a handful of 'Modern Rustic' rush-seated chairs, did nothing to emphasize the chapel's intimate and contemplative atmosphere, or to complement either the beautiful 14th-century carved and moulded screen or the 18th-century neo-classical mouldings on the wall monuments.

'The colour was key,' says Luke, describing the quality of the light, particularly at early morning prayer time, as an 'interesting blue'. Rachel Schwalm, an artist whose work lies between painting and sculpture with a healthy dose of technology underpinning it, was commissioned by the cathedral's art consultant, Sophie Hacker. 'When the sun's in that area,' continues Luke, 'the feeling you get in that space is there's a lot of blue in the light. It's the nature of the colours that tend to stand out.

'Rachel had some nice ideas about picking up the blues. She came up with a series of suggestions, notably a blue screen, very delicately done on an aluminium panel, which used LEDs coming into the panel from behind to make the whole thing glow. It created a powerful focal point in that space.

'The clergy kept asking her to come up with a design for an altar in which to mount it, but she was struggling.

BELOW The original altar – a wooden table covered by a simple cloth – was suitably humble but completely missed the suggestion of transcendence.

OPPOSITE The prayer desks and stacking benches continue the same moulding detail as the white stone shelf supporting an 18th-century neo-classical memorial plaque that can be seen in the background.

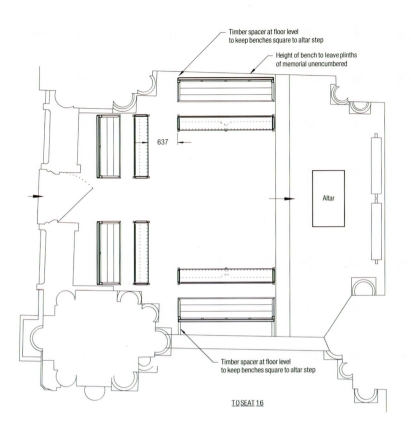

Timber spacer at floor level
to keep benches square to altar step

Height of bench to leave plinths
of memorial unencumbered

637

Altar

Timber spacer at floor level
to keep benches square to altar step

TO SEAT 16

OPPOSITE AND OVERLEAF Artist Rachel Schwalm's unearthly illuminated panel eloquently evokes transcendent spirituality, giving the small space unusual power as a retreat for private prayer. The stark lines of the square-cut Jerusalem-stone altar make the form retreat and keep the focus on the light.

ABOVE The layout of stacking benches and prayer desks (left). Strictly speaking, the chapel accommodates fourteen people, but the four-seater benches will seat five family members bunched together. Luke's own sketches for the chalice-like candleholders led to the finished objects, recalling Romanesque column capitals.

We were all committed to helping her come up with an altar that was going to be successful, but we needed to work very closely together. I love working with artists; it's always very exhilarating.

'I said, why not make it in stone, thinking we could get some – very appropriate – Jerusalem stone from a mason's yard in Pietra Santa, the Italian stone workshop we worked with on St Giles's in Edinburgh [page 78]. But it's the nature of stone to be rectilinear; it's a bad idea to try and get anything curvilinear or ornate to match the neo-classical mouldings, which Rachel had been trying to do. I said, this is nuts, we're not thinking about the nature of altars. They are tables to break bread on. If we need a focal point for prayer, then we need to leave the artwork to do the work, and the altar must be subservient to that. We just had to provide the frame to support her image; our ego needed to disappear. We kept it as simple as possible – just looked at the massing and proportions, and the ergonomics, then designed furniture you can sit on and pray at to link with the altar. It all had to hang together. But the altar itself is not the focal point, as it is in St Giles; rather, it's the panel.'

The four oak prayer desks and benches are restrained, 'done very carefully', says Luke, 'to scale and size to

make it work, leaving a monastic feel to the whole thing'. A simple blue inlay picks up the colour theme, and modest moulding details reflect the rich neo-classicism of the wall monuments. 'The resonances feel appropriate to the other languages going on in the building,' adds Luke. When lifting one of the benches, a pleasing practical touch – small but effective – is the indent in the bottom rail: carefully placed at the exact point of balance, it leads the hand to grasp it. Nothing is more annoying than lifting a piece of furniture only to find that it tips over in your hands.

The quiet, contemplative 'refuge' atmosphere of the tiny space is enhanced by the candleholders for the starkly rectilinear altar, designed by Sophie Hacker and Canon Roly Riem. Their form follows the visual theme of a Romanesque capital – the chapel's columns are 12th century – while the faceted bases provide the play of light and shadow that forms such a strong feature of the moveable altar in Bristol Cathedral (page 44). A few thoughtful moves, gently sensitive to context and bold where it's needed, have transformed the little chapel into a precious place of peace.

SHEFFIELD CATHEDRAL

Bench-marking: stackable mobile pews liberate a multifunctional space

'In two thousand years of ecclesiastical architecture,' says Luke, 'no one thought about stacking pews.' This pithy historical analysis leads us nicely into the story of Sheffield Cathedral's nave seating. 'In the beginning,' continues Luke, glossing cheerfully over when this so-called beginning actually was, 'there was no church seating. Churches were empty, beautiful stone barns. As soon as you put an altar in, it becomes a church. Such a piece of furniture symbolizes the building's use. That's the power of furniture: telling the story of how a building is used.'

But to return to the history of ecclesiastical furniture. According to Frank and George Barna in *Pagan Christianity? Exploring the Roots of Our Church Practices* (2008), 'The first backless stone benches began to appear in English churches in the thirteenth century, originally placed against the walls of the nave. Over time, they were brought into the centre of the room, first as moveable furniture and later fixed to the floor.

Wooden benches replaced the stone ones from the fourteenth century and became common in the fifteenth.' But Luke is right in saying that seating was not common in pre-Reformation churches, and that, until Victorian times, cathedrals were by and large devoid of seating. The reason why the redoubtable Jenny Geddes, one of those minor but memorable players on the early 17th-century historical stage, could throw her stool at the head of the minister in St Giles's Cathedral, Edinburgh, in high dudgeon – 'Daur ye say Mass in my lug?' – was that she had brought it with her.

'Until the Reformation,' says Luke, 'everyone stood in churches. They were designed to be seen empty. Only when the requirement arose to listen to sermons and not just be present for the raising of the Eucharist did the Protestant Church say, "OK, you can sit down now."'

In the Counter-Reformation of the 1620s, Archbishop William Laud required all churches to be 'pewed out', which led to the custom of families paying for their pew,

BELOW The dark, heavy, comparatively clumsy and unsociable Victorian pews that had to go. Not only did they make the interior entirely inflexible, but also they swallowed natural light.

OPPOSITE Looking towards the west end with its 1960s crossing, tower and open porch designed by Arthur Bailey. An abstract sculpture by Amber Hiscott hangs from the 'Modernist Gothic' lantern above the rows of Luke Hughes & Company stacking and linking benches in light oak, bringing light all the way to floor level.

RIGHT Careful attention is paid to achieving elegance for the stacking benches when they are actually stacked. This particular group is in St George's Church in Bloomsbury, central London.

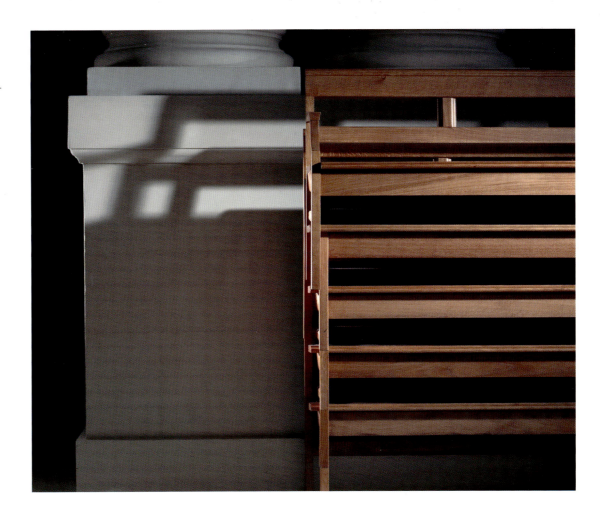

OPPOSITE Studies in light and shade reveal themselves when the sunlight streams through the cathedral's high, narrow windows. The arm detail can be seen in the upper image and the prayer desks in the lower, all neatly linked – as are the benches.

the closer to the front the better – and the more expensive. In a society where it was illegal not to attend church on a Sunday, the private pew conferred status in the parish hierarchy.

In major cathedrals, however, there was no seating until the late 19th century. At a time when timber-conversion technology amounted to no more than an unwilling youth on the floor of the saw-pit, and in the days before canals and railways, pews were expensive to make and difficult to distribute. Come the Industrial Revolution and the Great Exhibition of 1851 (which an adolescent William Morris refused to enter, driven by his horror of the ugliness of dehumanizing industry), and 'machines could churn out pews by the mile,' says Luke. 'They were expensive, but it was now possible to plane out industrial quantities of large timber pieces. It was much cheaper to make pews than chairs. The whole push with Victorian churches was to seat them out. It was a semi-political, Church and State phenomenon, driven by a growing population in need of paternalistic social engineering. There are always more church spaces than really needed.

'Why on earth no one thought about stacking pews is still a mystery, because the multi-functional community space that is the modern church was very much foreshadowed by those empty churches.' Pews locked down the seating arrangement, otherwise known as space planning, and consigned the ecclesiastical interior to inflexible single use.

'Our first pew – or bench – project was for St Barnabas in Dulwich, south London, in 1997,' says Luke. 'The budget was very constrained, and we found we could do a four-seater bench for more or less the same price as a single chair, with just a bit extra on materials. So it cut the unit cost per seat, and also a family of five can sit on a four-seater bench, which makes a potential 20 per cent increase in the capacity of the building. We ended up making the benches to fit the grid of the floor. It was easy to lay them out correctly, or stack and clear them away. They are light enough for most people to lift, but secure enough to stay stable.

'That's how we came to Sheffield. By then we had done eighty churches. We started with the pew seating in the nave – there was no flexibility. One of the things the client said was, "Look, this is an urban cathedral. Tramps come in and sleep here. We want them to be able to do that, and they can't do it on chairs."

'There was a lot of discussion about how to handle the benches. We took the client to St Mary's in Ealing and showed them our dolly system, which allows you to

stack benches up and move them five at a time. It was the way the dollies worked that completely transformed the space.'

With longtime colleague and photographer Tim Imrie, Luke set himself the challenge of stacking and moving Sheffield Cathedral's entire complement of benches for 600 people, plus prayer desks. It took the two men 17 minutes. 'That', says Luke, 'is putting the building to work.'

ABOVE Detail of the prayer desks fronting the rows of stacking benches. 'Quirk' details, sometimes known as 'cockbeads' – grooves or beads – are machined for decorative effect, but also to disguise gaps that open as a result of movement where panel meets frame or where the solid timber's width will show shrinkage.

OPPOSITE Modern oak furniture in an ecclesiastical interior – a far cry from the dark, heavy and gloomy pews usually associated with churches. Oak tells a story of longevity and strength, but it doesn't need to be stained the colour of coffee.

OVERLEAF The texture and colour of oak and stone combine to enliven the space, made more noticeable by the open structure of the benches.

ELY CATHEDRAL

Octagonal regeneration: eight hanging oak trees and hundreds of gilded eels

'It's one of Europe's finest architectural jewels,' says Luke of Ely Cathedral. 'As fine as you'll find anywhere.' The extraordinary cathedral, the 'Ship of the Fens' as it's known, dominates this ancient and idiosyncratic Cambridgeshire city of a mere 20,000 people. Perched on an 'island' 26 metres (85 ft) above sea level – the highest point for miles around – the city owes at least a part of its collective consciousness to isolation among the treacherous marshland that existed until fen drainage began in the 17th century. St Etheldreda founded the city and abbey in 673; construction of the cathedral began in the late 11th century and lasted until the dissolution of the abbey during Henry VIII's Reformation of 1539. The Octagon lantern tower, erected in the 1320s, is a staggering achievement, on a scale rarely found in British, or indeed European, cathedrals. It is the 'greatest individual achievement of architectural genius at Ely Cathedral', says Nikolaus Pevsner (*The Buildings of England: Cambridgeshire*, 2nd edn, 1970),

the kind of construction under which people stand gazing heavenwards, asking how on earth (or heaven) did they do that?

As a shape, the octagon has numerous religious connotations, including regeneration, transition and the relationship between earth and heaven. There is also a connection to another famous European octagonal church, San Vitale in Ravenna, from which Charlemagne took much of the marble and brought it back to Aachen, site of the throne whose distinctive sweeping arms influence Luke Hughes & Company chairs to this day, including the ones at Ely. The cathedral's huge octagonal tower – much wider than the original nave crossing, which collapsed in the 1320s, giving the impetus for the new structure – leads up to timber fan vaulting that appears to support the glazed timber lantern. But the lantern is actually held up by a complex timber structure above the vaulting, something that could not be built now simply because there are few

BELOW A visitor surveys the previous plinth and plain, rectangular 1970s supplementary altar in the crossing under the Octagon lantern's variegated light.

OPPOSITE 'How did they do *that*?' Constructed in the 1320s, the Octagon at Ely is the subject of many superlatives, especially Nikolaus Pevsner's, who called it the 'greatest individual achievement of architectural genius' at the cathedral. 'The Octagon is held up by eight oak trees hanging in the air,' explains Luke, obscurely, until it is understood that the soaring construction is supported from above, by enormous oak timbers braced into the verticals of the supporting tower stonework.

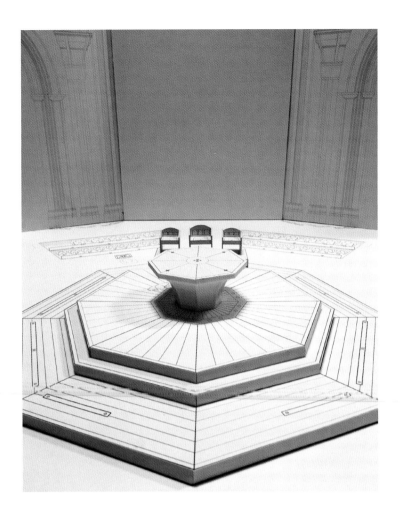

trees big enough. This is Luke's 'eight oak trees hanging in the air'.

'As an undergraduate at Cambridge,' says Luke, 'I remember visiting the cathedral often, and even then seeing the nave altar and furniture and thinking how disappointing it was and how wonderful it would be to replace it. Well, it took forty years, but here we are.

'The brief was to replace the nave altar and liturgical furniture, for which there was a design competition. I don't need to tell you how much I wanted to win it, after so many years. They needed an altar, its dais, clergy furniture and choir stalls, the conductor's stand, the credence table, and so on.

'The 1960s stuff they had – designed by George Pace – bore only a slim relationship to the building. And the choir stalls couldn't move because of these steel things stuck in front of the beautiful nave screen.' A hint of architectural inspiration is visible in the 1960s bishop's and clergy seating, but its clunky medievalism, complete with through tenons and scalloped sitting surfaces, utterly fails to reflect the soaring, transcendent elegance of the breathtakingly vertiginous space. 'The references had to be to the Octagon itself,' says Luke, 'as well as the muscular Romanesque arches of the nave.

'The scale is massive,' he continues, stating the abundantly obvious, but pointing out that, from a design point of view, 'Pretty much anything you put in there will either look silly or totally out of scale.' The company's preparation for the competition paid great attention to scale and massing: 'The architectural model we put in as part of the design submission showed we had really looked at the scale. And at the colours, as a matter of fact, which change throughout the day as the sun moves round. The crucial thing was to be able to get rid of it all. We had to make it disappear. All that furniture is stored in just two bays of the north transept.'

Central to the ability to store the furniture discreetly was the engineering element, particularly in the case of the dais for the octagonal altar, which, with its sixteen radial components and the central segment, measures a generous 9.35 metres (30 ft 6 in.) across. 'It's massive, but each component needed to be small enough to go through the gap between the arches in the north transept. We mocked it up in plywood and took it on site to test it, which gave us a good idea of scale as well.

'We worked with the artist John Maddison, who knows the building very well, on the colour. Colour is key

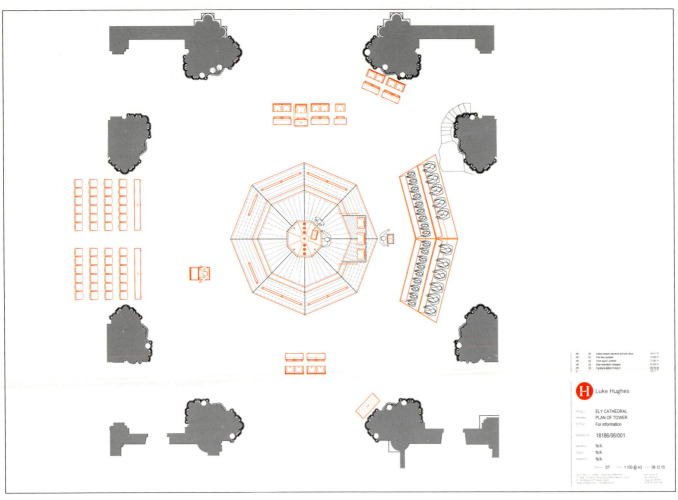

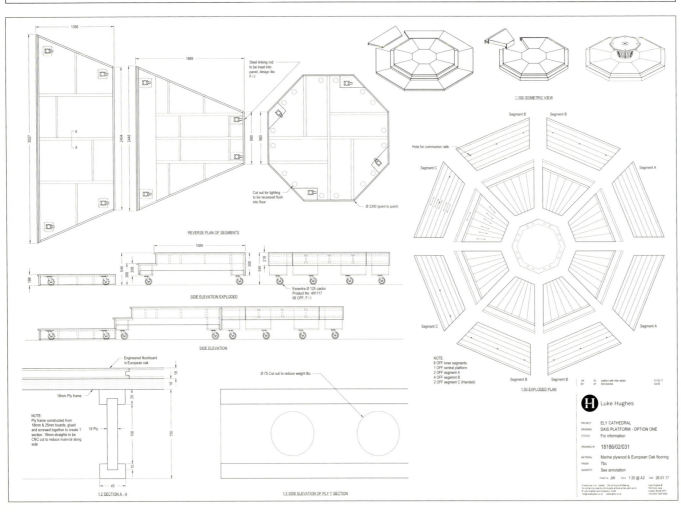

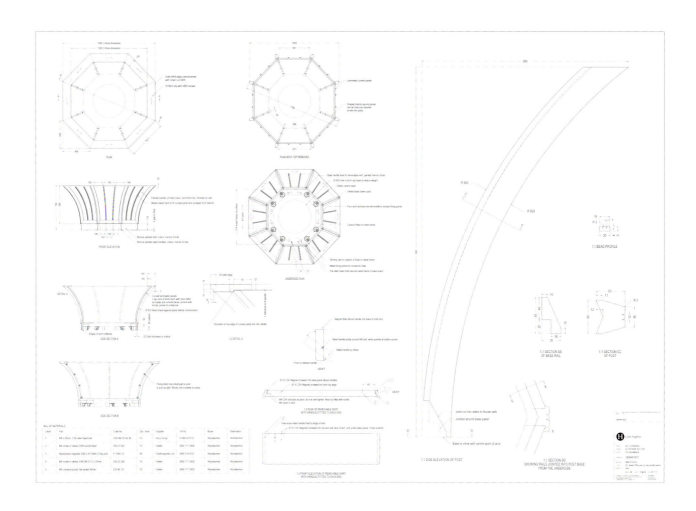

OPPOSITE Plan and layout drawing showing the location and organization of the proposed new altar and furniture (top), and a working drawing showing construction details of the engineered plinth components.

ABOVE Detailed working drawing of the altar itself – a woodworker's challenge if ever there was one – reflecting the inverted shape of the Octagon above through its outward-curving structural posts and a range of specially made fittings. The Arts and Crafts spirit abides, but this would have been well-nigh impossible without sophisticated design software and CNC (computer numerical control) machinery.

RIGHT Variations on the colour scheme for the altar, with the final choice at bottom right. The carved and gilded eels round the top edge shimmer and reflect the light, animating the space and making them visible from the west end of the nave 80 metres (262 ft) away.

ABOVE, TOP A Luke Hughes & Company designer waves from the top level of the plinth, seen here undergoing a trial fitting of the plywood components in a warehouse. A very large, column-free space is required to build something more than 9 metres (29 ft 6 in.) across.

ABOVE Carver Gyorgy Mkrtchian (left) created the eels that writhe around the top edge of the altar, reminding visitors of the original source of Ely's wealth. Cabinetmaker Matthew Smith (right), of Roland Day Workshop, clamps the complex collection of curves and angles that make up the altar's ambitious basic structure.

OPPOSITE Elevated view of the complete installation, with altar rails and liturgical furniture all in place.

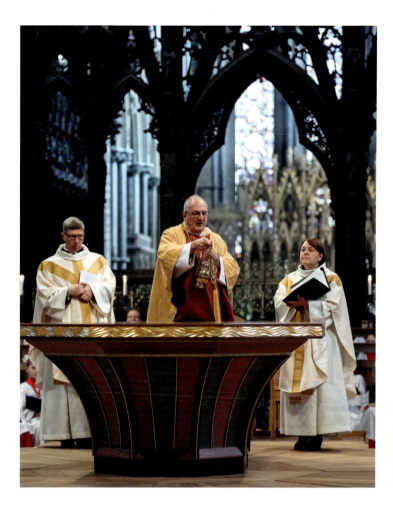

to the altar. The changes to natural light through the day are huge, but the references were already there from the stone floor. We developed that on to the altar to make it all hang together. We also needed to find a way of throwing light back to the west end, twelve bays down, so that, when you enter the space at the back, the altar is already the focal point.'

To achieve this effect, gold leaf was laid by Philip Surey on to Gyorgy Mkrtchian's carved, abstract figures of eels writhing around the altar's vertical edging. Ely's source of wealth in ancient times, eels made the abbey the second richest in England, as recorded in the Domesday Book of 1086, and (arguably) gave the city its name.

The clergy chair and choir stalls, being demountable, offer 'lots of permutations', including the ability to expand to accommodate visiting choirs. 'As always with our major projects, we need to create flexible space that can be used in lots of different ways,' says Luke.

'I love finding an engineering solution,' he continues. 'It's critical to me. You just unlock the whole thing with a flick of a switch – no tools. They're moving everything every day, sometimes three times a day. It makes the massive changes as easy as they can be. The underlying theme is the use of engineering techniques in wood

and steel to enable all these other things to happen. It all revolves around the architecture and how you inhabit that space to enable the building to work better. That's what we do.'

ABOVE The finished altar's meticulous craftsmanship and bold octagonal form reflect Ely's architectural magnificence at the same time as generating an affecting sense of the numinous.

OPPOSITE The bishop's chair and clergy stalls, together with all the other choir and liturgical furniture, can all be stored in two bays of the north transept. The massive Romanesque arched nave generates a perfect perspective sightline.

OVERLEAF As one looks east towards the high altar, the cool light through the stained glass counters the visual richness of rood screen and reredos. A close-up of the undersurfaces of the altar emphasizes the outstanding achievement in craftsmanship, delivering both richness and simplicity.

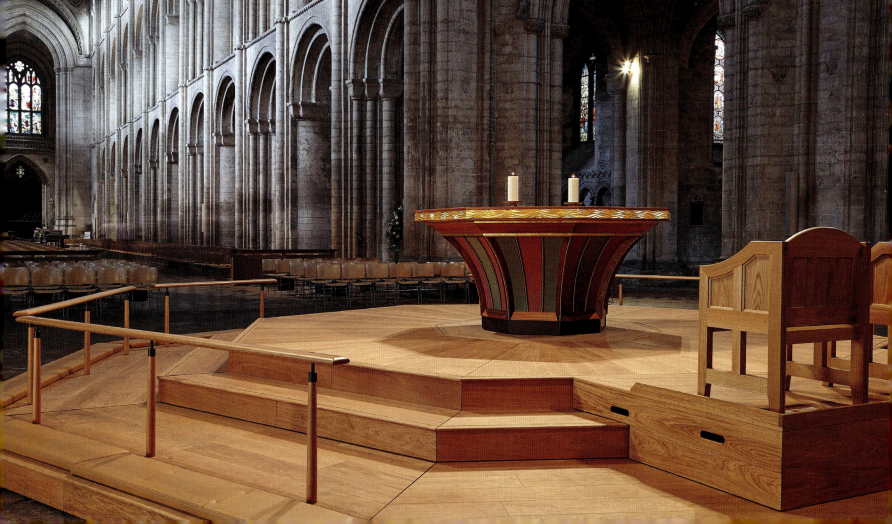

ST GILES'S CATHEDRAL, EDINBURGH

An ethereal Holy Table – a single block of vibrant marble – 'floats' in the shadowy interior

St Giles's Cathedral, also known as the High Kirk of Edinburgh, is the Church of Scotland's principal place of worship in the Scottish capital; it has also been the 'town kirk' for a thousand years. Far from the building being a relic, its congregation is lively and active, and it receives some 400,000 visitors a year. Since the 1980s, an ongoing renovation programme has included a sophisticated flexible lighting scheme, new stained-glass doors in the west entrance, a metal screen designed by the Icelandic artist Leifur Breidfjord, and careful restoration of an array of Victorian stained-glass windows.

The culmination of the effort was a commission for a new Holy Table, whose location had already been radically changed, in a return to ancient practice, to the 'crossroads' in the central sanctuary, directly under the fan vault. The existing table had been temporary for years, a humble wooden box covered with cloth, but not a 'real' altar.

The elders of the Office of Worship & Doctrine of the Church of Scotland contacted Luke Hughes & Company

because, says Luke, 'they'd seen what we had done in Bristol Cathedral'. The ensuing discussions about the shape and form of the piece were influenced by 'the tradition of the plain table', continues Luke. 'There could be no remote echo of the idea that this might hold saints' relics or anything that suggested Catholicism.' The then minister, the Very Reverend Dr Gilleasbuig Macmillan, who had been driving the restoration programme, wanted to make the sanctuary location permanent, and as the models and mock-up process evolved, it became clear that a single, solid, monolithic block would be the best solution for a number of reasons.

'When we mocked it up in MDF,' says Luke, 'a single cube worked better than any of the other ideas. The simpler the better. I particularly wanted it to "float" in the space' – a suggestion that met with universal approval from the elders. 'I was also conscious', adds Luke, 'that we had to get the entire assembly up the outside steps and place it absolutely precisely.'

BELOW, LEFT St Giles's, with its distinctive crown steeple, has been a cathedral in the formal sense of the word (i.e. the seat of a bishop) only twice since it was built, both times during the 17th century. For most of its post-Reformation history, the Church of Scotland has not had bishops, dioceses or cathedrals, meaning that the term 'cathedral' today carries no practical meaning. The 'High Kirk' title is older.

BELOW, RIGHT Interior of the nave with the 'temporary' Holy Table, a simple cloth-covered box, already in its new position under the fan vault.

OPPOSITE One plinth or two? This optical illusion is simply a reflection of the new Holy Table's brilliant white texture in the mirror-finish surface of the black Nero Marquinha marble below.

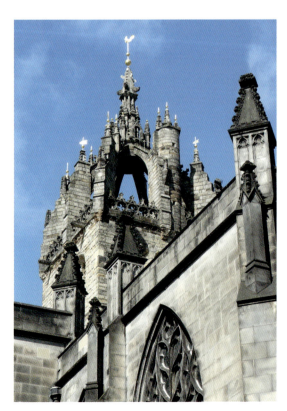

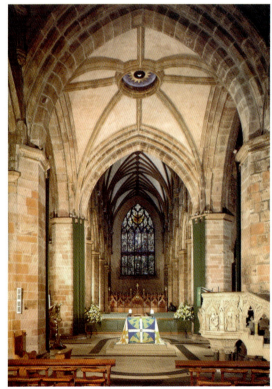

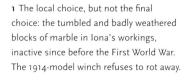

1 The local choice, but not the final choice: the tumbled and badly weathered blocks of marble in Iona's workings, inactive since before the First World War. The 1914-model winch refuses to rot away.

2/3/4/5 The Pietra Santa quarry near Pisa, land of Carrara marble. The scale of the machinery brings a gleam to Luke Hughes's eye; the saw blades in figs 3 and 4 are unlike anything ever found in a woodworking shop. In fig. 5, Pietra Santa's Mauro Rovai lends scale to the blocks themselves.

6/7 The hand-tooled texture on the vertical sides of the block took ten days to complete in the workshops of local mason Bertozi Felice. 'I knew we had to have texture,' says Luke. 'It wasn't apparent until we saw the single cube that it couldn't be all shiny.'

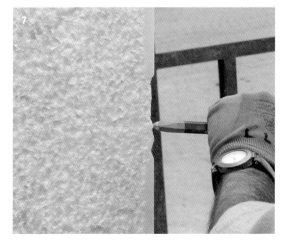

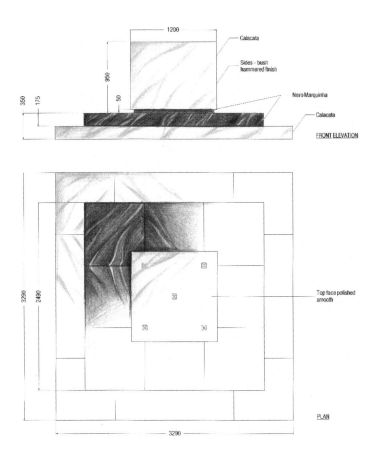

FRONT ELEVATION

1200 — Calacata

Sides - bush hammered finish

Nero Marquinha

Calacata

950

350

175

50

Top face polished smooth

3290

2490

PLAN

3290

ABOVE Plan and elevation of the new Holy Table *in situ*. The 'shadow gap' that generates the floating illusion is shown clearly; the Calacata block sits on top of an undersize slab of Nero Marquinha, severing it from any visual connection with the supporting slabs.

It remained to find such a block. Marble was the material of choice because of its luminescent quality, and the first research destination was the tiny Hebridean island of Iona, which St Columba used in the 6th century as a base to spread his brand of Christianity in the far north of the land mass that is now Britain. The marble workings there had been defunct since the First World War; and although large blocks still remained, they were so weathered as to be rendered useless. It would have been possible to re-open the quarry – although not, perhaps, to revive the 1914 machinery still on site – but overcoming the logistical challenges involved were beyond the budget.

The obvious next stop was the Italian town of Carrara, a name synonymous with marble, where the challenge of finding a single, 4-tonne block of the finest quality and completely without flaws was taken up by Mauro Rovai of the Pietra Santa quarries near Pisa. 'It was fun,' says Luke, 'running round the hills with Mauro and his monstrous quarrying saw looking for blocks.' The decision was finally made to use a brilliant white block of Calacata marble, which would float above a plinth and steps of Nero Marquinha, a black, white-veined stone, themselves set on another layer of Calacata.

'Dressing the stone was key to getting the rhythm and harmony of the whole thing,' says Luke, who had paid six visits to the quarry and workshops before the block was ready. 'I wanted it to gleam, to stand out as a focus of light in the rather gloomy interior. It needed to shine, but not with that vulgar sheen that you get in hotel foyers – it needed to throw light, not just shine. Once the block was cut and we saw the size of it as a single volume, I knew we had to have texture. I wanted the top to be smooth, but it wasn't apparent until we saw the block as a single cube that it couldn't be all shiny.' And thus the distinctive hand-tooled finish was developed for the vertical surfaces, the result of ten days' work with a diamond-tipped chisel by one of the craftsmen in the workshops of Bertozi Felice, close to the quarry. 'I was reminded of Michelangelo's "Prisoner" figures,' says Luke, 'emerging out of a single block.'

Once the black marble for the supporting plinth had been found – in a nearby quarry run by Mauro's two brothers – and the textured finish achieved, transportation and installation for more than nine tonnes of marble produced a new set of challenges. One of Mauro's team arrived from Pietra Santa with the stone and worked with local stonemason Nic Boyes, Arup structural engineer Bryan Edie and cathedral architect Graham Tristram. Various techniques for placing the Holy Table in its exact position were discussed, including the Renaissance sculptors' trick of setting a large and heavy object on blocks of ice that lower the object into position as they melt. Ultimately, the lifting and placing was handled by an 'ordinary' mobile crane, but even this process demanded true skill and craftsmanship to locate the block precisely and without damage.

Installed, the Holy Table exerts an uncanny luminescent force, attracting the eye in the low light of the interior. The supporting layer of Nero Marquinha stops short of the table's edges, creating shadow gaps ull round and generating the illusion that the table is floating. 'The effect is much more sophisticated than you'd think at first,' says Luke. 'The scale and re-setting of the steps are absolutely key in that process. You come in through the west door and really see the table just floating in the space. The light shines off it without being reflective, a great contrast with the sombre sandstone.'

The Holy Table was dedicated in the presence of the Princess Royal in January 2011 at a special service of thanksgiving. Roger Lindsay, Baron of Craighall, a Scot living in Toronto, was there to represent the Scottish Church Trust of Canada, which had made the generous gift of the table to the cathedral. Speaking at the service, Gilleasbuig Macmillan said: 'A national treasure such as St Giles's will always need the support of generous people. But this is an appropriate time to thank all those who contributed to and continue to support this great work of renovation. The congregation at this afternoon's service encompasses a wide spectrum of Scottish life and demonstrates how this cathedral has sat so centrally in the community throughout our history.'

BELOW The 4-tonne block of marble emerges from its wooden packing case, having been craned up the cathedral steps. Unprecedented care and precision were needed to lay it exactly square and directly under the centre of the fan vault.

OPPOSITE From a distance down the nave, the visual impact of the Holy Table is remarkable, lifting and lightening the whole space. The luminescent power and purity of the simple geometric form, undecorated and unadorned with cloth, cross or candle, is palpable.

OVERLEAF Handsome, tactile and with enormous presence: the table *in situ* is quite otherworldly, suggesting its spiritual and communal functions with great strength and beauty; the textured surface underpins the smooth polished top. Looking east past the choir, the interplay of predominantly blue light from the stained glass and the white of the hanging lanterns generates a glow in the Carrara stone. 'It needed to throw light,' says Luke. 'Not just shine.'

THE CHAPEL ROYAL OF ST PETER AD VINCULA AND THE CHAPEL OF ST JOHN, TOWER OF LONDON

Furniture in architecture; furniture in history

OPPOSITE The new clergy seating in the Chapel of St John, the Norman place of worship in the White Tower commissioned by William the Conqueror for his own private use in 1078. Note the scalloped seats and the curvature of the arms, after Charlemagne's throne at Aachen. The 'quirk details' – small-diameter mouldings on the edges of panels or structural components – provide light and shadow modelling and effortlessly conceal the expansion and contraction of the panels, which is inevitable in a damp atmosphere like the Tower's.

BELOW Woodcarver Gyorgy Mkrtchian, a regular collaborator with Luke Hughes & Company, rendered the story of St Peter ad Vincula – St Peter in Chains – for four panels in the ends of the choir stalls, using the chapel itself as an architectural backdrop. On the left is the real-life portcullis gate; on the right, the carved St Peter languishes before the very same door, chains and all, but with the portcullis closed.

The two chapels in the Tower of London are quite different propositions architecturally and historically, but their physical proximity, the similarities in the furniture families deployed in their refurbishment, and, perhaps most tellingly, the underlying cultural significances for Luke Hughes & Company – and indeed for Luke himself – render the two stories much more coherent as one. Or perhaps as two sides of the same coin.

The Tower itself does not rank in the 'top twenty global visitor attractions' list, its comparatively modest 2.8 million visitors in 2017 hardly holding a candle to New York's Times Square (35 million), Disney World in Florida (16.6 million) and even London's Trafalgar Square (15 million). But it is one of the very oldest, if not *the* oldest, of the ancient piles in which the historic heart of England still beats, and even 2.8 million visitors a year puts quite a strain on that venerable organ.

It is this core of Englishness that infuses the work of Luke Hughes & Company, and nowhere could it be more eloquently expressed than in the Tower. The resonances continue, with the company's significant portfolio of work for royalty – five royal palaces at the last count – and many more that have been opened or attended by Her Majesty the Queen. 'She has opened at least a dozen buildings we have worked on,' says Luke.

The particular brand of elastic and resilient Christianity to be found in the Church of England is another theme. Luke describes himself as 'Christian in a good old-fashioned, slightly agnostic sort of way', mentioning that his mother and maternal grandfather are Roman Catholics, and that his great-grandfather was Jewish. 'An awful lot of people who have expressed the best things about this country', he says, 'have been immigrants of one sort or another. Hughes, my stepfather's name, comes from Huguenot – none of your Welsh Huw's for me! But the story is bigger than me.'

Of course it is. But it is also true that of all the English furniture designers and makers living and

working in the early 21st century, none encapsulates these diverse and robust English traditions in quite the same way as Luke Hughes does, and that certainly none of them has his intellectual grasp of such traditions and the craftsperson's place within them.

And then there is English oak.

'English oak was the right material,' says Luke Hughes & Company designer Laura Tunstall. 'The Tower has a policy to use native materials where possible, and oak would traditionally have been used for generations.'

'Where English oak tends to be beautiful,' adds Thomas Barnes, of Luke Hughes & Company supplier Vastern Timber, 'is actually a product of poor woodland management. English woodland is more open, with more light coming in from the sides. You get pinpricks, swirls in the grain and flecks of colour. It creates a more interesting piece to look at. We don't often get to see where our timber ends up, what it turns into, so it's nice

to see pictures of the end product. The Tower of London is a testament to what you can do with English oak.'

The Reverend Canon Roger Hall, chaplain of the Tower of London, was the driving force in the 2014 refurbishment of the Chapel Royal of St Peter ad Vincula, which had last been fitted out in the 1960s. 'More than a million visitors a year for fifty years put severe wear and tear on the interior,' he says. 'The idea was to replace all the furniture, to enable us first and foremost to worship God in a place of worship of a very high standard, but also to serve the visitors who want to hear the history of the three queens – Ann Boleyn, Jane Howard, Lady Jane Grey – who are all buried in the chapel.

'Now it's all English oak,' he continues, with obvious relish. 'It's significant that every piece of furniture – the choir stalls, the altar and altar rail, the chairs, the lectern – is all made from the same wood. In 1965 every piece of wood was a different colour and a different type;

OPPOSITE In another of Gyorgy Mkrtchian's carved panels, St Peter unchained addresses a small group of entranced disciples, keys (to the Kingdom?) in hand. Behind him is the same fenestrated façade of the chapel that can be seen in the photograph on this page.

LEFT, TOP The south façade of the Chapel Royal of St Peter ad Vincula, built in 1515 and located in the Tower's inner ward. Three queens of England – Anne Boleyn, Jane Howard and Lady Jane Grey – are buried here, drawing nearly three million visitors a year.

LEFT, BOTTOM Luke Barton (left), the Luke Hughes & Company designer and project manager who worked on the St Peter ad Vincula commission, discusses one of the choir-stall end panels with Gyorgy Mkrtchian.

OVERLEAF Queen Elizabeth II with the Yeomen Warders of Her Majesty's Royal Palace and Fortress the Tower of London, and Members of the Sovereign's Body Guard of the Yeoman Guard Extraordinary – popularly known as Beefeaters, ceremonial guardians of the Tower of London. On the opening day of the refurbished Chapel Royal of St Peter ad Vincula, the Queen's ceremonial signing of the visitors' book and 'team photograph' were conducted on Luke Hughes Folio chairs.

there was no harmony. Now there is a complete sense of harmony in the place. The standard of craftsmanship is incredibly high, and it's very beautiful – absolutely stunning. The chairs are comfortable and of high quality, and there are the beautiful carvings on the ends of the choir stalls. There is an integrity, a real tone within the place, that was sadly missing before.'

Luke Hughes & Company's commissions for the two chapel interiors came hard on each other's heels, in 2014 and 2015, but 440 years separate the Norman Chapel of St John in the White Tower, built in 1078 as William the Conqueror's private chapel, and the Tudor St Peter ad Vincula in the Tower's inner ward, dating from 1515. St Peter ad Vincula (St Peter in Chains) is burial place not only to the three queens of England mentioned above, but also to a saint of the Catholic faith, Sir Thomas More – which gives the chapel special significance in the English religious tradition. Resonances were further amplified by the Queen's opening of the refurbished interior on the 100th anniversary of the outbreak of the First World War, and the installation of *Blood Swept Lands and Seas of Red*, an artwork by Paul Cummins and Tom Piper consisting of 888,246 ceramic poppies – memorable moments in the Tower's timeline.

The re-seating of the Chapel of St Peter ad Vincula (the first of the two commissions) included new bespoke chairs based on the original Coventry Cathedral chair designed by Gordon Russell's architect brother Dick, liturgical furniture, choir stalls and altar. Carved panels by Gyorgy Mkrtchian set in the ends of the choir stalls, featuring parts of the Tower as backdrops, tell the story of St Peter's escape from Herod's prison.

The Chapel of St John commission was to completely refurnish the interior, the aim being to evoke something of the building's original intent while still making it serviceable for the vast numbers of visitors (more than 450,000 in a single day during Easter 2017). New furniture included an intricate dais with communion rail, benches, stacking choir chairs, a storage chest, a lectern and a font, all in solid English oak.

The chapel is in one of the first Norman buildings completed after the Conquest, and was commissioned by William the Conqueror as a private place to pray and take communion with his family. 'Spiritually, I find it one of the most moving ecclesiastical interiors,' says Luke. 'What's more, this is probably the most important Norman building in the whole of England. It's incredibly significant. With so many visitors, the problem was how to retain the dignity of the space and still turn it round for services on Sundays.

'Chairs were simply not up to that, so we put in our benches. Plus visually, the seating needed to be robust enough to deal with that Romanesque interior. It has a kind of "oomph" to it, with those massive columns – incredibly muscular. There's something fantastic about the Romanesque and its simplicity. We were trying to say that we can do in oak something of what they were trying to do in stone.

'The key is to support the building, the architecture. It's always my mantra. How could we enable it to be relevant? Furniture defines the building's function, and the wrong furniture kills the building.'

Luke is justifiably proud of the installations in both chapels, perhaps with a little more than the normal frisson of satisfaction that comes from work that succeeds on all levels – appropriate design and materials, painstaking craftsmanship, and what one senses as a numinous, quietly spiritual quality. The finely judged details are expressive but never overbearing: the crenellated leg tops of the liturgical chairs in St Peter ad Vincula; the subtle curve of the chair arm in St John, reminiscent of Charlemagne's throne at Aachen; the hand-stitching of the leather footrests. 'Arts and Crafts? Yes, absolutely,' says Luke.

'It's a place of worship we are setting up for the next fifty years,' says Canon Hall, of St Peter ad Vincula. 'We want to leave a legacy for the people who worship, who come in on Sunday or for weddings, baptisms, carol services. It ties in with our mission and our hopes for the future. There will be a church still here and flourishing in the years to come.'

'I attended the St Peter ad Vincula opening and the First World War commemoration in November 2014', says Luke, 'and saw our Folio chairs, which we'd made fifteen years earlier for the New Armouries, set out in a row. Clearly it was going to be a team photo with the Queen and all the dignitaries sitting in my chairs. I wasn't asked to vacate – I was wearing a military tie so they must have thought I was security – and when the Queen arrived she went down to the crypt of St Peter ad Vincula, knelt and paid her respects, and signed the visitors' book. A heady moment of reconciliation between the Roman Catholic Church and the Church of England, all on my chairs. Never mind furniture in architecture, this is furniture in history.'

OPPOSITE The Chapel of St John. Luke Hughes & Company made the dais and altar rail, the lectern, the clergy liturgical furniture and the benches. The last of these needed to be robust enough not only to withstand the millions of visitors to the chapel, but also to complement the muscular Romanesque interior.

OVERLEAF The benches harmonize with the rhythm of the columns in the Chapel of St John. The clergy chairs in this chapel are simpler in decorative terms than those in St Peter ad Vincula. 'The stop moulding creates a termination point,' says Luke. 'It reads very clearly. The raised turned dowels through the joints have a very Arts and Crafts feel. It's a damp building, you can't rely on glue, so we peg them. But this is for fifty, sixty, even a hundred years of product life, so let's have two pegs and exposed dowels, the sort of thing Ernest Gimson or Sidney Barnsley would have done. The quirk mouldings on the panel edges mean they can expand and contract and the gaps get hidden in the shadows. It humanizes the inevitable. You've got to have it, so why not use it as a detail rather than pretend it's not there.'

CONGREGATION BEIT SIMCHAT TORAH, NEW YORK

Community, inclusivity, accessibility – and light

'I got an email completely out of the blue,' says Luke. '"Dear Sir or Madam, we understand you know a thing or two about liturgical furniture. We are designing a new synagogue and need someone to work up the designs for furniture into stackable units." Well, we've done this for more than a hundred churches, so I didn't see why we shouldn't do it for a synagogue.'

Thus began a project of considerable significance for Luke Hughes & Company, not least because, although the firm already had major US clients – notably the universities of Harvard and Yale – this project was of quite a different stripe. Here, the furniture would be used by a prominent lesbian, gay, bisexual and transgender Jewish congregation, in its new home over three floors (including basement) of the distinctive, 'Assyrian style' S. J. M. Building in New York, completed in 1928 to a design by Woolworth Building architect Cass Gilbert.

Founded in 1973 and catering for LGBT+ members from the city and beyond, Congregation Beit Simchat Torah – whose devotional functions are supplemented by community support and social and political activism – had been searching for a new home for some years. Stephen Cassell, of architects Architectural Research Office, had responded to the brief for a new sanctuary and memorial chapel with some elegant and inspiring design moves, especially the inclined, glass fibre-reinforced concrete wall that feeds daylight dramatically into the underground space.

The furniture brief was originally to develop existing designs and make them stackable so that the sanctuary space could be cleared and used for dinners, Passover Seders, bar mitzvah celebrations, weddings and other such events. The chapel, with its memorial wall dedicated to members who have succumbed to AIDS in the years since the congregation established itself in the 1970s, is a quieter and more contemplative space.

Luke's concern – as always – was that the furniture should not only reflect the architectural quality of the

BELOW Among Cass Gilbert's significant contributions to New York City's architectural landscape is this unusual, 'Assyrian style' loft building on West 30th Street for the fur trader Salomon J. Manne. Congregation Beit Simchat Torah's search for a new home ended here in 2011, and the radical remodelling of three floors was started in 2014. The dedication service took place in May 2016.

OPPOSITE The main sanctuary space, with the curved benches that form the corners of the seating area inspiring a sense of warmth, community and fellowship.

LEFT The original seating proposals for the sanctuary, as sent by the architect to Luke Hughes & Company as a starting point for the development of stackable versions. Note how the architect had been considering the length of the room as the main axis, and how this left an awkward shape for the congregation, many of whom would feel at a distance.

LEFT AND BELOW Luke Hughes's proposals showing the seating turned through 90 degrees and the addition of the distinctive curved benches. The key to the new layout's ability to bring the congregation into closer communication is the simple but powerful curve seen in the floor plan (opposite)

LEFT A render of the view towards the Holy Ark from under the soffit of the mezzanine. Each member of the congregation is near the ark in this orientation of the room.

scheme, but also enhance and express the congregation's core values of transparency, intimacy and flexibility. The architect, far from harbouring resentment over the entry of an upstart Englishman, was very happy to work with Luke Hughes & Company and its wealth of experience. 'A good architect understands we genuinely have something to bring to the table,' says Luke. 'We've been doing nothing else for nearly forty years.'

Early on, the decision was made to base the scheme on the company's principle of stackable benches. The design language then evolved, first through iterations with solid backs, and later with an open frame and rail treatment that would allow light to permeate the space.

The key driver for the success of the project, and a worthy technical challenge for the Luke Hughes & Company designers and partner workshops, was to make curved versions of these stacking benches. 'Not an easy task,' says Luke with characteristic

understatement. The process involved a fusion of traditional steam-bending techniques – not common for the notoriously inflexible oak – with digitally controlled three-dimensional machining.

The floor plan of the sanctuary space was thus turned on its axis, putting the bimah and pulpit on the long side of the room instead of at the end, so that the dramatic inclined wall would serve as a backdrop, and no member of the congregation would be more than 10.5 metres (35 ft) from the Torah reading or Rabbi's address. How the room layout works is shown in the plan of the sanctuary, incorporating two-, three- and four-seat benches, with eighteen of the two-seaters curved rather than straight. Plum-coloured velvet-plush upholstery adds visual and physical comfort, erasing the memory of 'those painful metal chairs', as *New York* magazine critic Justin Davidson described the former furniture.

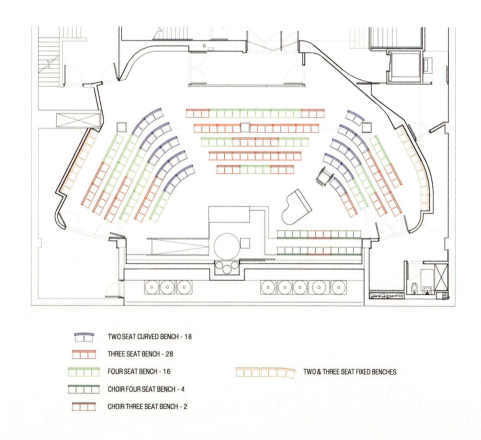

TWO SEAT CURVED BENCH - 18

THREE SEAT BENCH - 28

FOUR SEAT BENCH - 16

CHOIR FOUR SEAT BENCH - 4

CHOIR THREE SEAT BENCH - 2

TWO & THREE SEAT FIXED BENCHES

טוב להודות ליהוה

MAY THEIR MEMORIES BE FOR A BLESSING כד

OPPOSITE, TOP The main sanctuary space is flooded with the light that pours down the signature sloping wall, illuminating and focusing attention on the Holy Ark, and eloquently expressing the devotional but accessible atmosphere that is supported and enhanced by the open backs of the chairs and benches. It is very a much a room for people.

OPPOSITE, BOTTOM The chapel's sombre mood suggests quiet, solo contemplation, as befits the memorial wall dedicated to lost friends and family, but the dramatic canopy over the magnificent central panel adds exuberant scale.

ABOVE The curved benches, stacking three high, have their own custom-made trolleys.

OVERLEAF The vibrant atmosphere of the synagogue is very clear from this photograph of a devoted and animated congregation deeply engaged in worship. 'I really believe that this building is an extension of CBST's soul,' said Rabbi Sharon Kleinbaum.

The chapel was furnished with a modified version of the chair that Luke Hughes & Company had designed for Lincoln College, Oxford, and with a bespoke variant of the Athena folding table, used for meetings or folded up and stored in a rack specially designed to fit behind the wall panelling.

The response to the newly furnished synagogue, both among the congregation itself and in the opinion of the architecture critics, was not far short of ecstatic. 'I really believe that this building is an extension of CBST's soul,' said Rabbi Sharon Kleinbaum, who officiated at the service of prayers of dedication in May 2016. '[It] will be a place for us to grow in ways we can't imagine.' The critics were similarly enthusiastic, not least because there is such a strong appreciation in New York of the city's architectural heritage. Davidson's *New York* magazine review praises the architect for 'injecting much meaning into a modest space'. He continues: 'History and symbolism weave through the building in intimate ways ... and in the spots where it counts, custom luxury asserts itself – in the pews for instance, made in London by Luke Hughes, which are made of oak, for a durability that is symbolic as well as practical; curved to bring congregants as close together as possible; stackable so the room can be cleared for

dancing; upholstered not just for comfort' (referring again to those 'painful' chairs). 'Gracefully curved burgundy velvet benches' is how Marjorie Ingall in *Tablet* described the seating, while Stephen Cassell noted that they were 'made by the Queen's pew maker'. 'I couldn't stop taking pictures of [the room],' he added. 'It was such a beautiful mix of rustic and elegant, geometric-mod and traditional.'

'A wonderful thing,' says Luke. 'We were pleased to be involved. Great client, great architect, great project. A lot of fun.' Congratulations for Congregation Beit Simchat Torah also came from the then president of the United States, Barack Obama. Writing on the occasion of the prayers of dedication service, he said: 'For over forty years, your congregation has contributed to the Jewish community in immeasurable ways – opening its doors as a house of refuge to those in need and those who are often left in the margins ... As you come together on this special occasion and recommit to the values you hold dear, I wish you all the best.' A fitting high point to the project.

CHAPEL OF THE RESURRECTION, VALPARAISO UNIVERSITY, INDIANA

Two Modernist icons revisited

This story is one of continuity. An iconic post-war Modernist English cathedral and an equally iconic post-war Modernist chair design abide in spirit, if not exact verisimilitude, in the heartland of the American Midwest – Valparaiso, Indiana, where the private Lutheran University of Valparaiso has been located since 1859. The project also encapsulates the crucial connection between Luke Hughes & Company and the work of Gordon Russell Ltd, which itself formed the clearest link between the Arts and Crafts furniture of Ernest Gimson and the Barnsleys and the modern – and Modernist – 20th-century world of volume production.

Most enthusiasts for the craft genome in English furniture design will know the name Gordon Russell. Far fewer know the name of his brother Richard Drew (Dick) Russell, eleven years Gordon's junior, who, with his wife, Marian Pepler, succeeded in what design historian and critic Penny Sparke has described as 'formulating a peculiarly British brand of Modernism'.

Trained as an architect at the Architectural Association in London, Dick Russell took over the drawing office at his brother's burgeoning company in the late 1920s. His innovative designs for volume-produced Murphy radio cabinets in the 1930s and his 'holistic' approach to interiors and furniture, which treated them as parts of the same project, broke new ground in design practice. Likewise, his positions as design director of Gordon Russell Ltd and, from 1948 to 1964, professor of wood, metal and plastics at the Royal College of Art made him a key figure in the development of Britain's modern design industry.

What those furniture enthusiasts really like about the work of Dick Russell is the chair he designed for Coventry Cathedral. In 1951 Basil Spence had won the competition to design England's most symbolically significant public commission of the post-war years – the 'Phoenix at Coventry', a new cathedral to rise, as it were, from the ashes of the stark but elegant ruin of the old, destroyed by German bombs in November 1940.

PREVIOUS PAGES Interior of the Chapel of the Resurrection, Valparaiso University, Indiana, in 2016, shortly after the delivery of Luke Hughes's chairs. Nowhere is Luke's observation that a chair used in large numbers sets up a 'rhythm of quantity' better exemplified.

LEFT The exterior of the chapel (top), which is very much more than a 'homage' to Coventry Cathedral – and 20 per cent bigger. Architect Charles Stade, says Valparaiso's Professor Gretchen Buggeln, 'was aware' of the Basil Spence design, which was not completed until 1962. Valparaiso was dedicated in 1959. The clunky 1970s pine benches (bottom) were just too heavy and cumbersome to be easily moved for the chapel's various uses.

BELOW A machining drawing for the astonishingly complex curved, canted backrest of Luke Hughes's version of the Coventry chair. Digitally controlled machinery can produce a long, curved mortise-and-tenon joint (a curved, canted tongue-and-groove?) that is much stronger than the dowels used in the original, 1960 version.

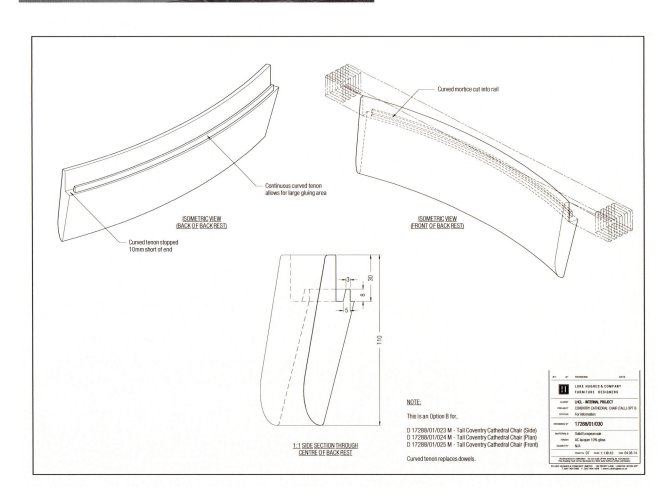

The commission was intentionally an occasion to celebrate art and craft: John Piper's magnificent stained-glass baptistery window, Graham Sutherland's giant altarpiece tapestry, and Jacob Epstein's St Michael and the Devil on the south-east entrance wall are all embedded deep in English visual culture. What also came with the new cathedral was a new sense of the need for versatility in the use of such a vast interior; so when it came to the furniture, pews were ruled out. Dick Russell's response to Spence's call for a truly British, Modernist, sturdy, stacking and linking chair that would speak the language of the 1,500-seat nave, as well as serve it functionally, became a classic, finding its way into cathedrals across the land.

'In 2012', says Luke, 'I got a call from Ray [Leigh, the former chairman of Luke Hughes & Company who had previously been chairman of Gordon Russell Ltd], saying he had been contacted by Professor Gretchen Buggeln, Chair in Christianity and the Arts at the University of Valparaiso, Indiana. She said they had a 1960s building, a "close match" to Coventry Cathedral, and wondered, since they were looking for new seating, whether they could use the Coventry Cathedral chair. Ray put her in touch with me, saying that, as a trustee of the Gordon Russell Trust Museum, he wasn't in a position to help,

but that if anyone could it would be me. It led to me going over to Indiana three times, meeting the decision-makers at the university and getting a feel for the building and how it now worked at the centre of university life.

'They'd put in long benches in the 1970s, but because they were so big and heavy they couldn't move them. The chapel is the main focal point of the whole university campus, and the Lutheran clergy, ministers and pastors wanted to use it for all sorts of things – morning prayer, concerts, plays, small private prayer groups – all of which needed furniture that could be reconfigured.'

As for a resemblance to Coventry Cathedral, Professor Buggeln's paper in the Lent 2010 edition of the university magazine, *The Cresset*, notes that '[the] comparison is indeed striking, particularly the monumental size of the buildings, the zigzag in the nave wall, and the similarities between our star-shaped chancel and the star-shaped "Chapel of Unity" at Coventry. Although this cathedral was not completed until 1962, Spence won the design competition in 1951, and his designs circulated widely. I am certain that Charles Stade (the Valparaiso architect) was aware of these designs, although the parallels are far from exact.'

Visits by the dean of the Valparaiso chapel to Coventry Cathedral itself and the Gordon Russell Design Museum in Broadway, Worcestershire, ensued. The design copyright became complicated because it resided with Dick's family, not Gordon's. Fortunately, through the good offices of Ray Leigh an agreement was reached that allowed Luke Hughes & Company to license the design from the museum, which had been granted the design rights by Dick Russell's estate.

'We spent a little bit of time', says Luke, 'trying to work out how to deal with the legalities, not least because Americans have grown a bit since 1959, and it was pretty clear that if we just put the chair into production at its original size it wasn't going to work. It was also frighteningly uncomfortable in ergonomic design terms. So our brief became to revisit the Coventry Cathedral chair, to re-engineer it, make it more generous, make it suitable for modern production techniques, improve the ergonomic performance and comfort, and make it work in the specific context of the chapel at Valparaiso – all this development with the say-so of the Gordon Russell Trust.

'But the university's leadership did realize that any chair they put in would completely influence or even destroy the design aesthetic of Charles Stade's "interpretation of Coventry Cathedral". They were very sensitive about it and were determined to get it right.

'When we got to the great moment of delivery and put in the new chairs they just looked right, as if they belonged. It was an extraordinary moment. Once again, the visual key lies in the rhythm of quantity.'

BELOW Floorplan of the chapel at Valparaiso. The star-shaped chancel owes a huge debt to Coventry's Chapel of Unity, although their positions on plan are different.

OPPOSITE The rhythm of quantity at work. The chair's legs carry a brass inset linking mechanism developed by Luke Hughes & Company, while the mechanically very strong 'planted' front leg joint has been re-engineered for yet more strength.

OVERLEAF Graduation at Valparaiso in front of Peter Dohmen's 'Munderloh' stained-glass window, which, although it pre-dates John Piper's iconic installation at Coventry, has a strong stylistic relationship to it.

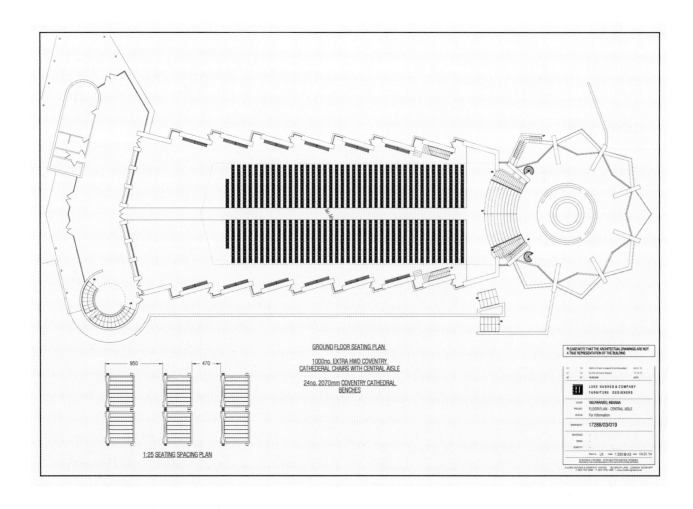

PLACES OF
WORK AND LEISURE

This section, although small in terms of the number of projects, runs the architectural gamut from A to Z and back again – with gusto. The British Embassy in Moscow (page 118) is an idiosyncratic, proto-postmodern attempt to add late-1990s 'Cool Britannia' pizzazz to Foreign Office tradition; Unilever House and the Diageo headquarters (page 124) present two sides of the corporate story, with 1930s neo-classical aspirations on one side and 1980s glass and steel on the other; the Supreme Court building (page 132), whose controversial conversion raised temperatures in the heritage lobby, is Edwardian late-Gothic mixed with Arts and Crafts and Art Nouveau touches; and Bury St Edmunds' Theatre Royal (page 150), the only surviving Regency playhouse in Britain, displays all the simplicity and elegance of carefully proportioned Georgian design.

Each of these different forms and typologies, in their different ways, gave Luke Hughes the opportunity to express, in modern branding parlance, the 'core concept' of Luke Hughes & Company – 'furniture in architecture'. The key design drivers, which are identified and developed very early on in the briefing process, are all different for each project, but all serve to show the humane but rigorous line of enquiry that the company undertakes to arrive at the ideal solution.

The story of the Moscow embassy is characterized by the yew tree that provided the timber for the ambassador's office; artist Norman Ackroyd, whose giant etching dominates the atrium, is constantly inspired by Wardour Castle – literally, as we saw in the introduction, next door to Luke's family home – and has spent many hours before his easel there.

The design challenge for the Unilever and Diageo office buildings, whose glass-topped and steel-framed furniture is emphatically appropriate for the slick, high-tech interiors, rested in cable management and getting process right so that on-site work was minimized.

The project for the Supreme Court – a 'slightly idiotic building' in Luke's affectionate phrase; he knows it well as his stepfather's place of work – was based on exhaustive research, including three days watching the law lords at work in the House of Lords, and a very tightly controlled specification. The library boasts a number of highly accomplished technical solutions.

The Theatre Royal is another project where furniture design overspilled into interiors, and which, most importantly, says Luke, involved 'sublimation of the ego. This beautiful Georgian building needed furniture that wouldn't scream for attention. If we got the furniture right, the economics of the theatre would work, which is a true undercurrent in all our projects. It's economic drivers that demand that benches stack or tables fold. Throughout our projects we are using furniture to enable the client to sweat the building as an asset.' Which is the Luke Hughes way: make the building work harder, ideally to the client's profit.

BRITISH EMBASSY, MOSCOW

Yew turn: the story of a tree

'Blair's new Britain has come to Moscow in the form of an angular, glass-fronted British embassy building,' wrote Amelia Gentleman in *The Guardian* on 18 May 2000. In the era of 'Cool Britannia', the previous embassy in a traditional 19th-century palace overlooking the Kremlin did not send the right messages of British creativity and forward-thinking to a fast-changing Russia. Ahrends, Burton & Koralek (ABK), the embattled but imaginative architects of the National Gallery extension pilloried by Prince Charles in 1984 as a 'monstrous carbuncle on the face of a much-loved and elegant friend', had come up with a quirky arrangement of towers and walkways in an airy, transparent structure. Standing among the architectural legacy of Stalinism on the Smolenskaya Embankment, four linked buildings house the chancery, offices, reception rooms and residential areas. The official ambassador's residence remained in the palace near the Kremlin.

But the real story of this project, says Luke, is a tree. A yew tree, to be exact. He is pointing out an obscure detail in one of the images hanging in the embassy's foyer, a 7-metre-high (23 ft) etching by the 'painter in acid' Norman Ackroyd. 'This copper etching here goes full height. It's really important. You see that building reflected in the water? It happens to be Wardour Castle in Wiltshire.' The texture of the Ackroyd etching, even in a low-resolution photograph, is palpable – and the stand of yew trees to the east can just be made out.

'In the early 1990s', says Luke, 'we did a number of projects for the Foreign Office – the embassies in Buenos Aires and Washington DC, the Nairobi and New Delhi high commissions ... at the time there was budget for an incoming ambassador to put new furniture or decorations into his or her new post.

'Richard Burton of ABK got in touch, and said he wanted to work with us – we had been recommended

by the Foreign Office – to develop designs for the furniture for the ambassador's and chancellor's offices in the new Moscow embassy. But he said, "I'm fed up with the usual timbers that everyone uses. Ash, beech, cherry, oak, maple, walnut. Haven't you got anything a bit more exotic?" "Well," I replied, "we have got some yew, as it happens. Came down in the 1987 storm."

'Richard got quite excited by this and asked me to bring some more ideas to the next meeting. The tree had blown down ten years previously in the grounds of Wardour Castle. It lay on the ground for eighteen months and nobody did anything about it, so I called English Heritage [the administrators of the 14th-century monument] and said, if I clear it, can I have the timber? They said, yes, what do you want to use it for? And I said, I don't know.' Yew, with its characteristic 'purple patches' of impacted and interlocked curly grain, differing colours and hardnesses, and short trunk

lengths, is notoriously difficult to work, certainly to achieve planks of any significant length.

'So I delivered some designs to ABK', continues Luke, 'and at the next meeting told Richard we had enough yew for the ambassador's office furniture – his desk, meeting table, bookshelves and so on. We also designed a suite for the chancellor's office, but that was in maple. Richard liked what we had done with the designs, and wanted to show me some of the artwork they had been commissioning for the embassy under the '1% for Art' rule [by which 1 per cent of the building's project cost was spent on art]. There was a glass wall by André Beleschenko, some of Robin Day's Gatwick Airport chairs, a Tess Jaray rug ... and a maquette by Norman Ackroyd. "He wants to send it all the way up, seven metres high, in the main foyer," said Richard. I looked at it, and said, "You know you asked me about the English yew? Well, the tree we're using for this furniture comes from there" – I pointed – "and I

BELOW Wardour Castle (left), the 14th-century pile in whose shadow Luke Hughes grew up, with one of Norman Ackroyd's many etchings of the castle to its right. In an instance of 'uncanny synchronicity', an ancient yew from the stand of trees in the castle grounds (bottom left) provided the raw timber for the ambassador's office furniture.

OPPOSITE The final version of the 7-metre-high Norman Ackroyd etching in the embassy's atrium lobby. The artist works directly on to the metal, in this case copper.

LEFT Desk and meeting table in the ambassador's office, high above the River Moskva. The glass top of the desk is fritted so that any papers resting on the 'courtesy shelf' below can't be read upside down by inquisitive visitors.

LEFT AND ABOVE The suite in maple for the chancellor's office, a much cooler and more rectilinear design, which suits the blonde wood better. The metal bracing pieces on the leg frames and the pronounced overhang to accommodate the pedestal are reminiscent of the early Oxbridge desks that appear later in the book (page 166).

BELOW The sparse structure of the large low table for the ambassador's office is designed to carry all the weight and stress of the substantial, 35-millimetre (1 3/8-in.) glass top through to the lozenge-shaped legs, whose veneering presented such a challenge to master craftsman John Cropper.

live there" – I added, pointing at the wall of my house visible in the image. "My dear chap, you can't be serious!" he said. "We must tell the Foreign Office." And so we had this strange element of uncanny synchronicity about the whole project.'

The yew – and indeed the design of the ambassador's desk – had further contributions to make to the story. The desk design incorporated three-dimensional curves that had to be veneered with yew, not an easy task at the best of times. 'John Cropper made it,' says Luke, 'who I think is one of the best makers, if not the best, in the UK.' But his workshop is in a North Oxfordshire farmyard and the job was going through in the dead of winter. 'He couldn't get the glue to go off,' says Luke. 'It was too cold and wet. So he took the vacuum cleaner from the house, and his wife's electric blanket. He then made a suction-bag veneer-press with the vacuum cleaner, and warmed it with the electric blanket so it would set. Absolute genius.'

A TALE OF TWO TABLES

Systems design for fast-changing corporate interiors

Or, to be more accurate, a tale of two table *systems*. Luke Hughes & Company's move away from the residential and retail markets in the late 1980s and early 1990s coincided with a flurry of major signature-architecture projects in London for big corporate clients. Two such clients were the drinks multinational Diageo, newly inhabiting a glass-and-steel behemoth on the Park Royal Guinness Estate in north-east London, next to Giles Gilbert Scott's 1933 Guinness Brewery; and, at the northern end of Blackfriars Bridge, the consumer-goods giant Unilever, occupants of Unilever House, the curved façade and giant Ionic columns of which have given that part of the Thames Embankment its imposing character since the early 1930s.

The tale of the tables themselves – two ranges with stainless-steel frames and tops in a variety of materials named Mercury and Curzon – is one of development, of exercising the same craft attitudes as with oak, cherry or walnut, of 'smart' design ideas that ensured flexibility and cost savings for the client, and of cable management, the major office-design headache of the 1980s and 1990s. 'The point', says Luke, 'is materials and process rather than product or client.' It is also very much about installation

'We were trying to find a design language that was very different from anything else on the market at the time,' says Luke – a language that would fit, for example, the typically 'high-tech' architecture of Kohn

BELOW An early iteration of Mercury, clearly showing the attempt to create a distinct visual relationship with the cast-aluminium four- and five-star bases of the premium office chairs of the time. Cable management at this stage is vestigal.

OPPOSITE A glass-topped oval version of Mercury in one of the Unilever House meeting rooms. The vertical cable-management tubes underneath expanded over time to take ever-fatter cable runs.

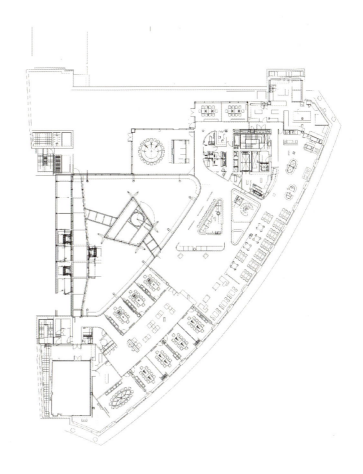

OPPOSITE A Mercury table in Unilever House, the laminated top sandwiching a layer of special stainless-steel mesh. The foot is designed to pivot round, thus throwing the angled supports outwards and creating a wider radius of support for an added leaf – which increases the width all round yet keeps the oval shape.

ABOVE The neo-classical Art Deco tour de force that is Unilever House, a 1933 London landmark on the north side of the River Thames. The design credits are shared between Unilever board member James Lomax-Simpson and architects John James Burnet and Thomas S. Tait. The radical 2004 refit by Kohn Pedersen Fox opened up the interior to create a vertiginous atrium, firmly wedded to the high-tech steel-and-glass approach.

OVERLEAF An added oval 'rim' in walnut has increased the overall size of the Mercury's top by 25 per cent, and its seating capacity from ten to sixteen. Note how the legs are angled outwards from the feet, as opposed to the inward orientation of the example shown on page 126.

Pedersen Fox Associates' Diageo headquarters. However, as is now common knowledge, such buildings as Diageo's HQ, as well as, more famously, Paris's Centre Pompidou and the Lloyd's building in London – of much the same vintage – depended for their uncompromising, engineered steel-and-glass aesthetic on painstaking handwork.

It is just the same with stainless-steel tables. Luke is enthusiastic about his 'brilliant' steelworkers, Sheetfabs in Nottingham, a company that, to his mind, is a persuasive embodiment of the Arts and Crafts principle of men becoming dignified by the very act of making dignified work. 'Working in stainless steel is very different from mild,' he says, 'not least because of what happens when you heat it. It distorts, so you have to deal with the jointing in a way that minimizes the distortion. Then what's really crucial is the polishing. It's done entirely by hand, especially on underframe structures as complicated as that. It's like the Pompidou – a machine couldn't produce the machine finish they wanted, so it had to be hand-done. Just because it's steel doesn't mean it's an industrial product. It's just like wood, requiring a very high degree of craft skill.'

Both table ranges were used in the Diageo and Unilever jobs, and both were developments of designs

that had been generated some time before. Mercury was originally designed in collaboration with the architect Ian Sharratt, then at Michael Hopkins Architects, for Pearson's corporate fitout in the mid-1990s; Curzon, essentially a simpler design, was originally conceived for the DTZ building in London's Curzon Street, hence the name. 'We'd gone on evolving the designs,' says Luke, 'but not for a specific job. We created the Mercury brochure as a marketing tool aimed at architects and got the Diageo project (with Aukett Swanke as the interior designer) because we had already developed the design from the initial concept into something more sophisticated and easier to make. It's the same refinement process as developing a chair. A new design language very different from anything else on the market didn't alter the fact that it had to be beautifully made. The skill required to make it gave it the quality that defined it.'

Key to the development of both designs was the cable-management capability, which had become a dominant element in all office-desk and table design since the 1980s (and which now, with the advent of wireless Internet and charging, has become more or less obsolete). 'Glass tops', says Luke, 'meant it was crucial to conceal or render the cable management

somehow visually acceptable. It became more and more elaborate, with sheaths of cable reaching fifty or sixty millimetres in diameter, and the standards seemed to change very year – 'Cat 4' to 'Cat 5' to 'Cat 6' to '6e'. Each time the standard changed, all the cable had to be stripped out and replaced. If the furniture wasn't structured to enable that, the client had to go out and buy new tables and desks.

'With projects like this, the key to success is designing out some of the problems you get on site before you get *to* the site. Having people on site is expensive, so you design for the absolute minimum of hassle.' Hence the development of a fully cable-managed Curzon table into a kit of parts assembled with an off-the-peg turnbuckle system that eliminated the need for any tools at all and radically reduced installation time on site. 'You're actually designing process. The installation and cable-management costs are about the same as the table itself. It's a "blind cost"

that the client just has to meet willy-nilly. If we were clever with the design and used our brains, the client would save – but we needed to demonstrate that it *is* clever design.'

Cable management or no, both designs have stood the test of time. 'I went round Unilever recently,' says Luke. 'They had smashed one of the glass tables and we were looking at replacing it. The project had been in place for ten years but the tables looked so fresh, modern and ... well, just *right*. I was bowled over because sometimes when at last you put a project into place you think, I hope that's the last I hear of that. But going back over this one, it still looks right. It hasn't dated; it's looking like a real classic.'

BELOW The Curzon design in two of its earlier iterations, with tops of different timbers. As with Mercury, the range could be customized to suit a top of almost any material, and there is also a range of height-adjustable and pivoting tops for people who prefer to work standing up.

OPPOSITE, TOP One of the meeting rooms in the Diageo headquarters dedicated to rare single-malt whiskies, complete with a bird's-eye maple-veneered sliding-top table. Each of the meeting rooms above a certain level is furnished as a tribute to one of the company's many drinks brands, using colour schemes and furniture choices that reflect the nature of the tipple.

OPPOSITE, BOTTOM Mercury again, its distinctive foot detail peeking out from the irregularly fritted glass top, which has been given an effervescent feel to conjure the tingle of a gin and tonic – made with Gordon's, of course.

THE SUPREME COURT, LONDON

'We define the law round here'

There is a beguiling narrative charm to Luke Hughes & Company's work for the Supreme Court, the highest court in the United Kingdom, located since 2009 in the governmental heart of London in a building that used to be Middlesex Guildhall. 'The building sits just across Parliament Square,' says the Luke Hughes brochure, 'which is now, with a quaint constitutional symmetry, ringed on one side by the State (in the form of the Houses of Parliament), God (in the form of Westminster Abbey), Mammon (in the form of the Treasury) and now, with the opening of the Supreme Court on the west side of the square, the Law.'

In architectural and urbanistic terms, the building has been the subject of much impassioned debate, but its particular resonance for Luke comes from the fact that he is of legal stock. His 'Pa', as he calls his stepfather, sat as a circuit judge in the Crown Court that was housed in the same building in the 1970s, while his great-grandfather, the first Baron Schuster, who served as permanent secretary to the Lord Chancellor's Office between 1915 and 1944, became 'one of the most influential permanent secretaries of the 20th century' (Jean Graham Hall and Douglas F. Martin, *Yes, Lord Chancellor: A Biography of Lord Schuster*, 2003). It was Claud Schuster, says Luke, who first articulated the idea that 'we ought to have a supreme court' in 1911.

It took nearly a century. The Constitutional Reform Act 2005 established a supreme court in law, transforming

BELOW Ornate animalistic carvings by Henry Charles Fehr occur throughout the building, whose criminal courtrooms were furnished in 'high ecclesiastical' mode. Note the pioneers of English law enforcement on the panel above the leather seats (top left).

OPPOSITE The highly decorated front façade of the building, designed by James Sivewright Gibson in 1912 as the guildhall for the county of Middlesex and repurposed as a Crown Court in the 1960s, where Luke's stepfather sat as a judge. The architecture critic and conservationist Gavin Stamp claimed its Late Gothic style is enlivened with 'a delicious Arts and Crafts – almost Art Nouveau – vigour in the details and sculpture'.

LEFT, TOP AND BOTTOM, AND OPPOSITE
The old Crown Court interior and
examples of the carvings by Fehr, whose
subjects ranged from Don Quixote to
rare and mysterious beasts, mythical and
otherwise. Nikolaus Pevsner called the
building 'Art Nouveau Gothic'; in Luke's
opinion, 'it doesn't know if it's Arts and
Crafts or Gothic Revival'.

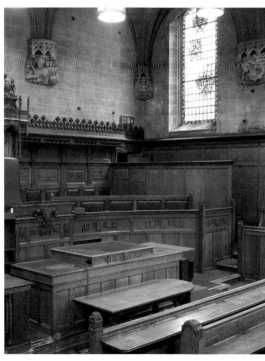

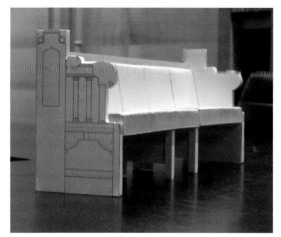

LEFT An early card model of one of the
benches, much like a church pew, whose
seats and backs were entirely remade
to save room, but whose carved and
decorated ends were preserved.

the age-old but constitutionally precarious system of appointing what were effectively supreme-court judges to the House of Lords, where, known as the law lords, they might well vote on legislation that they themselves had passed. A supreme court would separate these powers – an anomaly at the heart of one of the world's oldest parliamentary democracies – and, more prosaically, it would need a building close to the seat of government. The decision was made to repurpose the Edwardian Middlesex Guildhall on Parliament Square, which had become a Crown Court in the 1970s. A supreme court, which concerns itself strictly with subtle matters of jurisprudence and the ongoing evolution of the law of the land, does not operate like a criminal court, whose layout and furniture must serve the adversarial system of plaintiff, defendant, prosecution and defence, so the idiosyncratic interiors needed to be completely redesigned.

Luke, who 'knew the building rather well' as his stepfather's place of work, is without sentiment – or even sympathy – in his opinions. 'It's a slightly idiotic building,' he says, 'with this ridiculous heraldry. It doesn't know if it's Arts and Crafts or Gothic Revival. There was all this incredibly elaborate pseudo-Arts and Crafts decorative stuff, lots of lovely little carvings that everyone was keen to conserve and thought would be stripped out.' The conservationist lobby had plenty to say about the scheme, much of it in the Ruskinian language of passion and outrage. 'What the Lord Chancellor proposes', fumed Marcus Binney, president of SAVE Britain's Heritage, in a campaigning leaflet of 2006 entitled 'The Guildhall Testimonial – Stop this Folly', 'is a disgrace, an example of needless destruction and waste which no other owner of a listed building, public or private, would be allowed to contemplate.'

OPPOSITE Two views of Court 1, the largest in the building, intended to accommodate nine justices; courts 2 and 3 serve five. American black walnut was used in courts 1 and 3 to harmonize with the existing stained-timber interiors. The benches kept their revived end-carvings but were reduced in size.

BELOW End detail of a curved justices' desk in American black walnut, and the interior of Court 3, which enjoys an abundance of natural and artificial light. Carved angels contribute to the strong ecclesiastical atmosphere.

The main focus of the ire was the interiors, the brief for the remodelling of which was already being prepared at the Department for Constitutional Affairs, shortly to become the Ministry of Justice. Nikolaus Pevsner reputedly characterized the building as 'Art Nouveau Gothic', referring perhaps more to the extravagant carvings by Henry Charles Fehr – who worked closely with the building's architect, James Sivewright Gibson – than the building itself. 'Gibson's Guildhall is remarkable not just because it is an Edwardian public building that is Gothic rather than Baroque, but also because its Late Gothic style – a complement both to the Abbey and to Parliament – is enlivened with a delicious Arts and Crafts – almost Art Nouveau – vigour in the details and in the sculpture,' wrote the architectural campaigner Gavin Stamp in 'Stop this Folly'.

Thus we have an Arts and Crafts connection, however faint, in another Luke Hughes & Company

project, albeit one that was beginning to look like a poisoned chalice – Arts and Crafts style or otherwise. The job came to Luke because of the company's work for the Edinburgh Law Library, the viewing of which prompted David Hope – the first deputy president of the Supreme Court – to insist that he and his fellow law lords 'didn't want anything less'. It was perhaps one of the most challenging and complex of all Luke Hughes & Company projects, not only because of the very public controversy that the decision to use the Guildhall had generated, but also because, as Luke explains, 'all the furniture needed to be sympathetic to the building' yet deliver an environment in which a legal process entirely different from the one for which the interiors had been designed could be carried on efficiently.

The scope of work amounted to a complete refurnishing of three courtrooms, one to accommodate nine justices and two to hold five (two of the three

Court 1 in session, with the work of nine Supreme Court justices (formerly law lords) supported by a range of judicial assistants, advocates and registrars. A provision to seat eleven justices – as used in September 2019 during the hearing to decide on the lawfulness of Prime Minister Boris Johnson's extended prorogation of Parliament – was part of the original brief.

Court 3, showing the justices' desk in silky black walnut, with the substantial document pedestals creating a kind of cockpit for each justice. The original radii of desks and seating were adjusted and, in the case of courts 1 and 3, moved through 90 degrees.

rooms being exemplars of the hybrid Arts and Crafts/ Art Nouveau/Gothic styles already discussed, the third being refreshingly modern); the library, which needed to house no less than 35,000 books and therefore required a bold architectural move even to create the space, never mind furnish it; and private offices for the justices and their assistants.

Feilden+Mawson were the architects appointed to execute the masterplan drawn up by Foster + Partners. 'They were a good team', says Luke, who clearly enjoyed working with them, 'and took care of all the conservation issues plus the space planning.' It was Feilden+Mawson's idea to cut through two floors down to the basement cells so that the library, now on three floors, could become both the physical and the intellectual heart of the building.

There followed eighteen months of painstaking research – including time in the Royal Courts of Justice

library, the library of the Judicial Committee of the Privy Council, and three days in the gallery at the House of Lords, where Luke watched the law lords at work. A minutely detailed specification was developed that left absolutely nothing to interpretation, however sensitive or accurate. 'We worked with Tomoko Azumi on the early concepts and then developed everything down to the very last detail,' says Luke. 'Everything was there. We left no room for anyone to cheapen the spec. We made all the prototypes and managed quality control during production.' The library shelves and fittings were made by EE Smith Contracts in Leicester, 'which took in our drawings very well', while most of the courtroom furniture was produced by Opus Magnum in London.

'It brought together for us', continues Luke, 'everything we had learnt about libraries, and everything we had learnt about managing tricky space.' There was a lot of discussion about IT issues and the televisual

BELOW An early model for Court 2, the modern one, which shows positions for seven justices. The final version accommodates five.

OPPOSITE All the installed furniture in Court 2 is European oak, much lighter than the black walnut used in courts 1 and 3. The quotations etched in the glass wall echo a theme that runs throughout the project, especially the library.

qualities of the spaces, and, above all, about the management of paper. The courtrooms had to accommodate the justices, judicial assistants, advocates, assistant advocates, registrars and assistant registrars. 'We rebuilt all the historic benches in the old courtrooms,' says Luke, 'which were originally designed on a radius. We replotted the radii to suit the new layouts and kept the original bench and desk carved ends, so we were able to re-use all the carvings.' The design of the seating in between the ends was all new. 'We knocked all the benches apart and then scarfed the joints to remake them, but narrower because they weren't going to fit into the rooms otherwise.' Courts 1 and 3 had been reoriented through 90 degrees in order to seat the required number of justices.

The library brought its own specific technical problems, not just the housing of 35,000 books in

a space that could barely hold 25,000. 'No one wanted to touch the original panelling,' says Luke, 'but we had to cram everything in. We actually had just five fixing points for all this shelving, to make sure the panelling wouldn't be damaged. We double-stacked the books on the shelves, and left the backs off the bookcases so you can look through and read the historic inscriptions on the panelling. We also managed to be a bit clever with the library lighting: after being thrown upwards, the light is reflected back down to the books.' These lights also carry the sprinkler system, something the mechanical and electrical engineers maintained couldn't be done, but which Luke and his team nonetheless achieved. The triple-height space, now adorned with selected quotations on law and liberty carved by Richard Kindersley, is redolent with the warmth and studiousness that characterizes the best libraries, and with which no conservationist could possibly find fault.

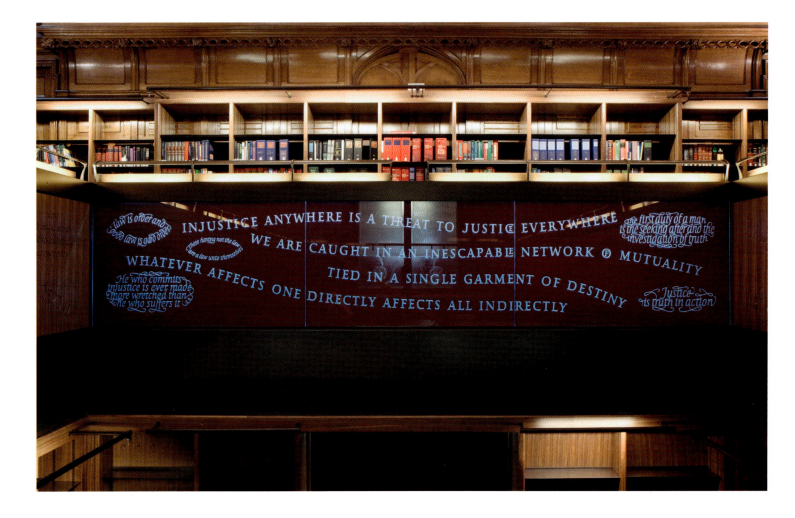

OPPOSITE The library staircase's balustrade carries further instances of Richard Kindersley's carved 'letters of the law', a detail of which is shown below. The library ladders – a necessity when 10,000 more books had been crammed in than the space could comfortably hold – were a health-and-safety concern for the Ministry of Justice, but not for the justices themselves, who bridled at the implied 'institutional senility'.

OVERLEAF The custom library shelving in American black walnut has only five fixing points back to the wall, as well as open backs so that the original panelling is not obscured. The strip lighting above the shelves also carries the sprinkler system, an achievement in the face of the mechanical and electrical engineers' insistence that it couldn't be done.

Despite the double-stacking of books, there was no alternative to filling as much of the height as possible with shelving, which required ladders. But this became a problem for the fledgling Ministry of Justice, 'which is just about as Orwellian as the name implies,' says Luke. The law lords, soon to become Supreme Court justices, decided to hold informal 'user group' meetings with Luke to chart progress, and were brought up short by the ministry's objections to the ladders on the grounds of health and safety. 'We can't use steps?' they responded. 'What, do they think we are institutionally senile?' 'The ministry is telling us they want 35,000 books,' Luke told the group, 'but the room is only a certain size, and we can only get a certain number of bookcases in.'

'We had ladders in college,' said David Hope, the law lord who had demanded something as good as Edinburgh Law Library. 'Ladders define the essence of library space.' Luke clearly enjoys retelling the story. '"What shall I say to them about the health and safety laws?" I asked them. They looked at each other, and one of them nailed it: "We define the law round here."'

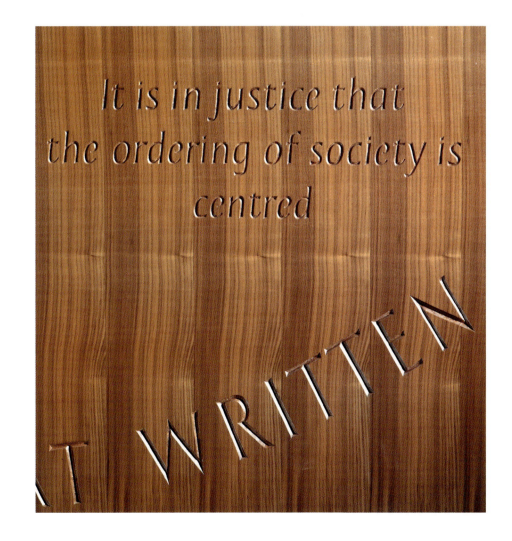

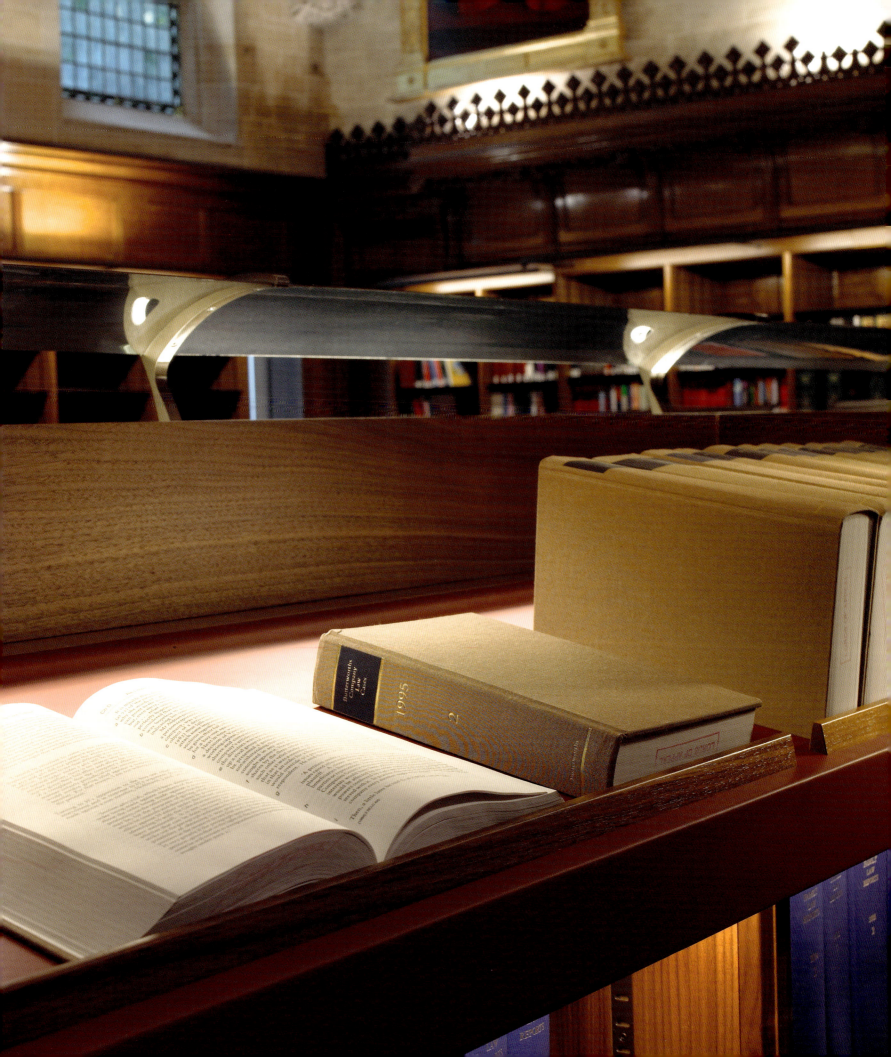

THEATRE ROYAL, BURY ST EDMUNDS

An adaptation for the stage

It's not often that an architect owns a chain of theatres; in fact, in the 21st century, at least, it's unheard of. It was probably no more common in 1815, when the neo-classical architect William Wilkins, best known for the National Gallery in London and Downing College, Cambridge, inherited his father's 'Norwich circuit' – a collection of small theatres in East Anglia, a region of south-east England. The coastal towns of Yarmouth, Ipswich and King's Lynn were 'outliers' to the regional agricultural hubs of Bury St Edmunds and Colchester, and the cultural zenith of Cambridge.

Wilkins opened the Theatre Royal, Bury St Edmunds, in 1819. 'It has always been a very popular theatre,' says Luke, 'especially with actors, who love the Georgian forestage that puts them right in among the audience.' In fact, the Grade I-listed building is one of only three surviving theatres in Britain, and the only working one, that give us a taste of what the early 19th-century theatregoer could expect for his or her entertainment. Wilkins's company of players toured all six venues, each of which was open only for a couple of short seasons a year, until the troupe was disbanded in 1843. Half a century of struggle and difficulty followed, brightened only by such theatrical highlights as the world premiere of Brandon Thomas's three-act farce *Charley's Aunt* at Bury St Edmunds in 1892. The Theatre Royal closed in 1903, re-opened in 1906, was bought by the local brewer Greene King in 1920, and ceased operating as a theatre, in the face of competition from the town's two new cinemas, in 1925.

The enthusiasm in the 1960s for restoration brought it alive again, and in 1975 Greene King, although still owners of the freehold, gave the theatre to the National Trust to preserve. Led by architects Levitt Bernstein, the £5.3 million restoration was started in 2005, and Luke Hughes & Company got the call that same year. The

BELOW AND OPPOSITE The sensitive restoration of the only remaining Regency theatre in the United Kingdom by architects Levitt Bernstein won a string of awards. Painstaking care was taken to revive all the original detail, including the lettering.

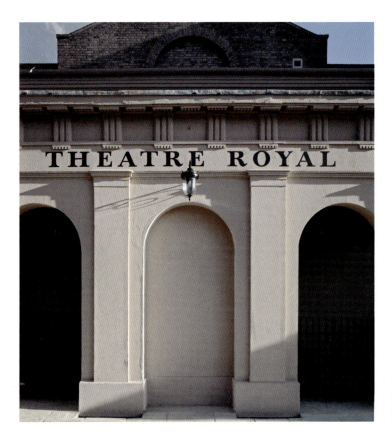

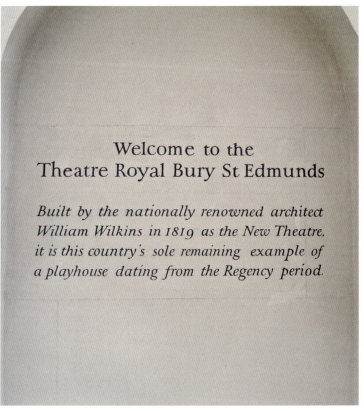

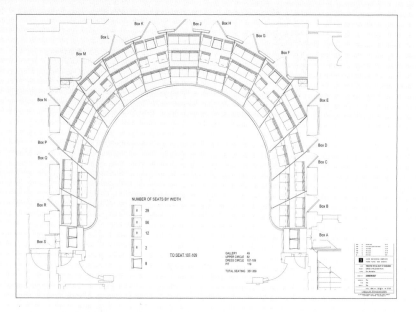

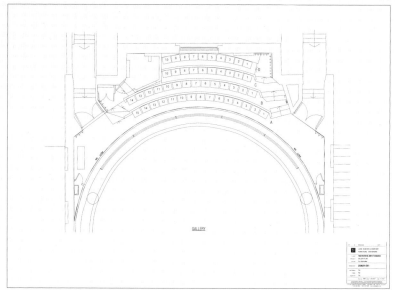

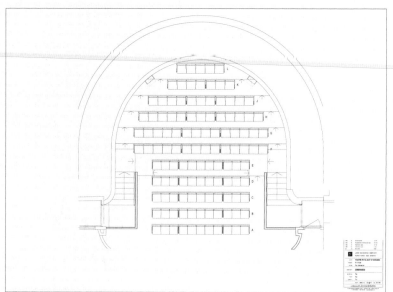

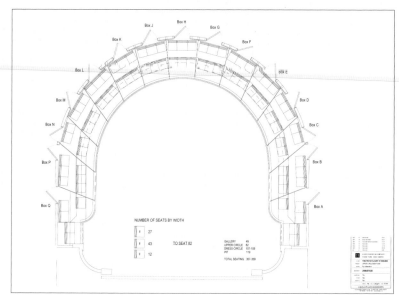

ABOVE Seating plans of the four levels
(clockwise from top left): dress circle,
gallery, the upper-circle boxes and the
stalls. The new installation increased the
capacity of the tiny theatre by fourteen
seats, delivering a significant increase
in revenue over a season.

ABOVE Work in progress. Lettering artist Philip Surey renders the seat numbers in suitably period style (bottom left); perplexed project teams grapple with access and logistics problems (top row); the Polish installers are satisfied with their work (bottom right).

original Georgian entrances to the 'pit', or stalls, and the boxes in the dress circle had been removed, while the seating layout had been entirely changed. 'They wanted to go back to the original theatre,' says Luke. 'The aim was to return to a working theatre, but very much as it would have been in Georgian times.' It was the perfect opportunity to revive not only the original architecture and layout but also the decorative scheme, as well as, indeed, the repertoire and stage techniques of the late 18th and early 19th centuries, creating an authentic experience in both historical and dramatic terms. The refurbished theatre opened in September 2007 with a performance of Douglas Jerrold's 1829 nautical melodrama *Black-Eyed Susan*.

Luke Hughes & Company replaced or revived all the seating; the plush tip-ups in the pit gave way to straight, three-seater bench versions of the company's Academy chair, originally designed for the Royal Academy of Music in 1990. 'It was one of first serial lines of chairs we did,' says Luke, who makes a policy of re-engineering existing designs. 'They wanted a theatre seat that looked like a bench, something quite neutral. Comfortable, but not a bucket-type seat. The simplicity is very obvious; it's all about the direction and patterns in the grain, and subtle detailing. It happens to suit that particular kind

of architectural form.' Versions appear in a radiused layout in the restored boxes in the two circles; the humble wall-mounted tip-up 'jump seats' up in the gallery got a cosmetic makeover.

'What we were trying do,' continues Luke, 'was create a workable seating option for a Grade I-listed building that had the National Trust and the theatre management company as client and tenant. We had to deal with the health-and-safety and fire regulations and so on – a very great difference between what was OK in 1819 and what the requirements are now. We didn't have much to play with in the budget; we had to enable it to be seating without drawing attention to itself as seating, to make it disappear.

'The geometry was key, as indeed was sublimation of the ego. This beautiful Georgian building needed furniture that wouldn't scream for attention. If we got the furniture right, the economics of the theatre would work, which is a true undercurrent in all our projects. It's economic drivers that demand that benches stack or tables fold. Throughout our projects we are using furniture to enable the client to sweat the building as an asset.

'There'll always be a role for the clever solution, because you have to use brains not only in the concept

but also in the process – how to make at a sensible price. All the Arts and Crafts principles are still in play, appealing to the brains of designers and makers to enable the architecture to happen.' Which is why the theatre's management were delighted to discover that the new arrangement had space for up to nine seats in some of the boxes, where before there had been only six. In a theatre that holds only 360 people, observes Luke, 'it made a big difference to the revenues.'

ABOVE The Academy chair, generous in width and designed for fifty to a hundred years of hard use, suited the proportions and geometry of the theatre. This is a stacking version. The installation images show the Royal Academy of Music (top) and St George's Church, Brandon Hill, Bristol.

OPPOSITE The rich palette of the colour scheme, complete with heroic neo-classical symbolism and a skyscape ceiling, ensures a genuine Regency experience for theatregoers. The theatre's repertoire is taken from the same period.

PLACES OF
LEARNING

This 'Places of Learning' group of architectural projects that Luke Hughes & Company has furnished includes far more new buildings than the 'Places of Worship' group. This gives a different emphasis to the fundamental Luke Hughes & Company philosophy of 'furniture in architecture', in that the relationships with architecture and architects are more creative and more clearly defined. The simple reason for this is that the architects in question are alive and working, and fully appreciate the Luke Hughes & Company working method.

Here, Luke is speaking about the Sainsbury Wellcome Centre for Neural Circuits and Behaviour (page 214), designed by Ian Ritchie Architects: 'Although there's very little in the building that is like anything else we've done, the intellectual approach is the same. It's about making the building work. It all comes together in a way you would never have expected without a really good client and a really good architect. This is what I enjoy with these problems. We haven't got the money, so we have to use our brains ... to synthesize everything we know, and then make something better than everyone expected. That's the joy of it.'

Joy indeed. Working with such architects is clearly what leaves Luke and his team feeling so fulfilled, and each project is approached with the same levels of professionalism and craftsmanship. 'You have to respond,' says Luke. 'The core story is to take what the architect did ... It's the same principle for dealing with very different architectural forms. The job is always to make the building work better.'

Many of the projects in this section can be described as interior, rather than just furniture, design. For Luke, interior design is about cushions and curtains – a wholly arguable position considering his company's space-planning skills – but he sees himself as an anthropologist. According to Luke, the dining hall at Oxford's New College (page 236) 'is not interior design. It's really about understanding how people inhabit these spaces. The only way I can describe it is social anthropology. Whatever is being done in a building, our process focuses on how to do it better. And it's all dependent on this collective lump of stuff we call furniture.'

On this subject, as on others, the Keystone Academy Library in Beijing (page 222) provides a final and very persuasive word. Painstaking research, commissioning and collecting artworks, using evocative colours and inspirational window panels of sophisticated typography, turning difficult interior elements to the advantage of the whole design – this is what interior designers do. But by and large they don't design and make highly crafted and engineered furniture with a product life of fifty to a hundred years. Perhaps we can call the design practised at Luke Hughes & Company 'total design'. It certainly works.

QUEEN'S BUILDING, EMMANUEL COLLEGE, CAMBRIDGE

Not just furniture in architecture, but furniture as architecture

'This project was one of our first truly collaborative design processes with a major London architectural practice,' says Luke, 'and it opened lots of doors when people realized what we could do. Michael Hopkins Architects themselves wanted to make the furniture part of the architectural whole, but it ended up being much more part of the architecture than anyone expected.'

The building itself, sitting as a hidden gem behind the Master's Lodge and expressed in the same beautiful, buttery Ketton limestone as Christopher Wren's neighbouring college chapel, is an unusual, free-standing oval, resting on a formal colonnade whose pre-stressed and post-tensioned columns act in the same way as the buttresses of a church.

The defining feature is the auditorium, seating 120 people on tiered benches with an upper gallery encircling the oval performance or lecture space. This is where the architects were struggling to make their idea work, particularly with regard to the integration of

writing tablets, as specified in the brief, and where they needed someone to work with in order to develop it. Luke recalls a number of official deputations from the college and the architects visiting his tiny Covent Garden workshop, where he was making 'endless mock-ups'. 'The benches were complicated because the back had to work as both handrail and support for the writing tablets, and the fire regulations were very precise about distances and angles.'

The 'big idea' for the benches was to make the writing tablets detachable, entirely without any mechanical movement. 'I didn't want rise-and-fall mechanisms,' says Luke. 'They're complicated, easy to break, require maintenance and you have to commit to left- or right-handed fitting. The driver of the whole design was that it would be completely service-free in perpetuity.' Formed of laminated veneered plywood, the tablets simply hook over the steel handrail and are held in place by their own curve, which holds the smaller,

BELOW Michael Hopkins Architects' beautifully proportioned, lozenge-shaped building sits tucked away in a quiet corner of the college grounds, the distinctive golden limestone recalling Christopher Wren's nearby chapel.

OPPOSITE The moulded and laminated ply writing tablets, held on the stainless-steel seating rails by nothing more than a secondary curve and their own weight, are a testament to the simplicity and ingenuity of bold design thinking. Fire regulations demanded extreme precision in the rake of and distance between the bleacher-style seats.

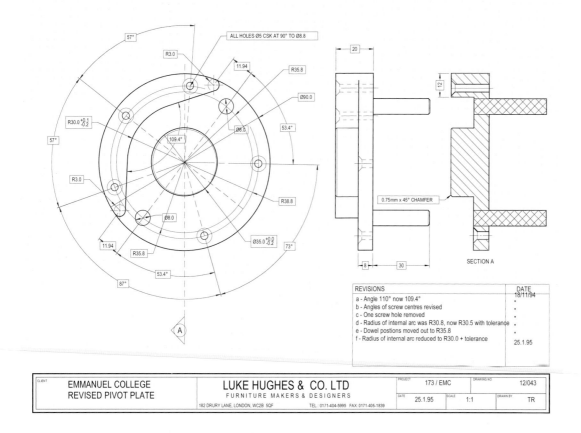

ALL HOLES Ø5 CSK AT 90° TO Ø8.8

57°
R3.0
11.94
R35.8
Ø90.0
R30.0 +0.1 -0.2
57°
109.4°
Ø6.0
53.4°
R3.0
R38.8
Ø8.0
11.94
Ø35.0 +0.0 -0.2
R35.8
73°
53.4°
87°

A

20
12

0.75mm x 45° CHAMFER

8   30

SECTION A

REVISIONS	DATE
a - Angle 110° now 109.4°	18/11/94
b - Angles of screw centres revised	"
c - One screw hole removed	"
d - Radius of internal arc was R30.8, now R30.5 with tolerance	"
e - Dowel postions moved out to R35.8	"
f - Radius of internal arc reduced to R30.0 + tolerance	25.1.95

CLIENT EMMANUEL COLLEGE REVISED PIVOT PLATE	LUKE HUGHES & CO. LTD FURNITURE MAKERS & DESIGNERS 182 DRURY LANE, LONDON, WC2B 5QF TEL : 0171-404-5995 FAX: 0171-405-1839	PROJECT 173 / EMC	DRAWING NO. 12/043
		DATE 25.1.95 SCALE 1:1	DRAWN BY TR

Detailed working drawings showing the componentry and mechanism of the tip-up seats lining the gallery. Following the same principle of ultra-simplicity in all moving parts, the block-laminated seat units are carefully balanced so that their own weight provides the tipping momentum. It all pivots on the crucial nylon bush, which sits atop the steel stanchions bedded into the concrete-floor substrate. The 'service-free in perpetuity' aim to minimize mechanical complexity, and hence maintenance, has been emphatically achieved: no springs, no counterweights, no complications.

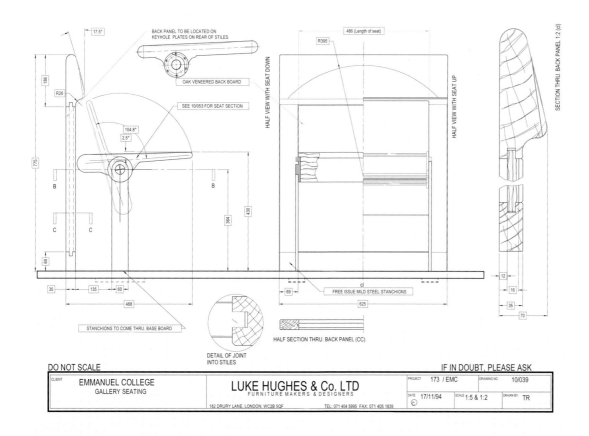

17.5°
BACK PANEL TO BE LOCATED ON KEYHOLE PLATES ON REAR OF STILES
OAK VENEERED BACK BOARD
186
R26
SEE 10/053 FOR SEAT SECTION
104.8°
2.5°
775
B   B
364   430
C   C
69
35   135   60
468
STANCHIONS TO COME THRU. BASE BOARD
DETAIL OF JOINT INTO STILES

486 (Length of seat)
R395
HALF VIEW WITH SEAT DOWN
HALF VIEW WITH SEAT UP
SECTION THRU. BACK PANEL 1:2 (d)
69
FREE ISSUE MILD STEEL STANCHIONS
625
HALF SECTION THRU. BACK PANEL (CC)
12
16
35
70

DO NOT SCALE   IF IN DOUBT, PLEASE ASK

CLIENT EMMANUEL COLLEGE GALLERY SEATING	LUKE HUGHES & Co. LTD FURNITURE MAKERS & DESIGNERS 182 DRURY LANE, LONDON, WC2B 5QF TEL: 071 404 5995 FAX: 071 405 1839	PROJECT 173 / EMC	DRAWING NO. 10/039
		DATE 17/11/94 SCALE 1:5 & 1:2	DRAWN BY TR

The tip-up seats in the gallery, showing clearly how the backrests are an integral part of the window and ducting assemblies. The college chapel can be seen through the windows.

secondary rail underneath. The auditorium is used for concerts and performances that don't require tablets anyway, and the storage is a simple, elegant vertical rack from which the tablets can be easily taken and put back.

The second 'big idea', of which Luke is justifiably proud, is the tip-up seats lining the gallery. 'The windowsill forms the back of the seat, which itself is on stanchions bolted into the concrete slab rising through the wooden floor. The whole thing pivots on the nylon bush, which again is as simple as it can be and entirely bomb-proof. We spent a great deal of time specifying the exact weight of the rear section behind the pivot so that it tips on its own, without any springs, catches or other complications.' Twenty-five years later, the interior – service-free in perpetuity – is still as satisfyingly handsome and functional as on day one.

The epilogue to the story comes in the shape of a grand piano. Someone, somehow, had forgotten that the piano needed to be brought into the upper-storey space for concerts and performances, and taken away again. Careful examination of the floor in front of the two central sections of the two front rows of raked seating reveals a discreet trapdoor. 'Those two sections', says Luke, 'separate and roll forward on conveyor-belt rollers, so the college can get their piano in and out through the trapdoor.' An afterthought, but an elegant one.

OPPOSITE AND ABOVE The interior's materials palette of oak, steel and leather generates a studious but comfortable atmosphere. Once a design decision has been made to eliminate moving parts, the process generates its own elegant solutions. Writing tablets are needed only for lectures, whereas the auditorium is used for concerts, recitals and much else. The loose tablets are stored on mobile 'dollies', picked off and hooked back on again as people enter and leave.

OVERLEAF From this angle, looking towards the rear of the auditorium, the exposed roof structure adds a workman-like quality to the space. The edges of the 'grand piano trapdoor' panels can be seen in the floor, front and centre.

A TALE OF THREE COLLEGES

Oxbridge's crucial contribution to Luke Hughes & Company's design, marketing and production strategies

Since 1990 Luke Hughes & Company has provided furniture for more than sixty of the seventy colleges that make up the universities of Oxford and Cambridge, amounting to some 2,500 rooms. The work is an exercise in generating and adapting a successful formula whose design parameters are as much about useability, longevity, logistics and minimized maintenance as they are about craft or aesthetics.

Britain was not a comfortable place for a small business in the late 1980s and early 1990s, Thatcherite monetarism had bitten deep into both corporate and personal spending power, and Luke Hughes & Company's retail business, which depended on its Ovolo bedroom-furniture range (page 17) – as sold through Heal's and similar outlets – had more or less completely stalled. 'We built off what we had learnt from Ovolo about bedroom furniture', says Luke, 'when we stopped supplying retail in the mid-1980s. The market had collapsed; no one was buying anything. We did a number of conference centres, for example for Courage Breweries and ICI, and some hotels. All the time we were learning how to design so we could get product not only out of the factory but also up the stairs or into the lifts. We were getting better and better at logistics.'

But there remained the problem of replacing the retail business with another client group. 'We identified the Oxbridge market as a result of the depression in the 1990s', says Luke, 'and started knocking at the doors of the colleges. Margaret Thatcher's policies had reduced university-grants money to a trickle, and conferences and student-fee income, especially from foreign graduates, who are in residence all year round instead of the twenty-four weeks for undergraduates, became key ingredients in balancing college books. They needed to look carefully at how they were generating revenue from their buildings, and the obvious areas were dining halls, libraries, accommodation and lecture theatres.

'We did a number of accommodation-block projects, the three most significant of which were Newnham and Pembroke colleges in Cambridge, and St Hugh's College, Oxford – all of them with new graduate accommodation, designed by architects who understood the relationship between architecture and furniture, and who recognized the value of

craftsmanship's ability to humanize their buildings. We developed a design language that was consistent with all that.'

Newnham's Rosalind Franklin block in 1995 was among the earliest of the Luke Hughes Oxbridge-accommodation projects, the company having furnished the college's dining hall only a year before. Allies & Morrison's design, a well-mannered response to the red brick and pitched roofs of Basil Champneys's original 'domestic collegiate' style, needed furniture for sixty bedrooms. 'What we did', says Luke, 'was to come up with a simple kit of parts. We designed for a fifty- to eighty-year life expectancy, and very deliberately made the furniture feel as if it were part of the building. We made it very light and simple, maximizing the light in the rooms, and extended that principle to the hanging shelves with open ends, both letting the light deep into the space and giving the occupants a resting place for their knick-knacks.

'Everything was well made in solid wood, all the drawers properly jointed, and so on. We reckoned the more we could get the furniture off the floor, the easier it would be to maintain the rooms. We removed the "Blu Tack factor" by providing a good-quality pinboard so the college didn't have to redecorate every year. We designed everything for easy maintenance, and didn't put any modern ironmongery on doors and drawers – the sliding mechanisms as well as the handles – because it goes out of date and can't be replaced. Everything in wood.

'We also researched how people actually behave in their rooms, which is why there are no tub chairs. Students don't sit in tub chairs; they just drape clothes over them. They like to use chaises longues in all sorts of different ways, so we designed a whole set of variations that they can lounge or curl up on. And we gave them lots of hooks – an inexpensive way of keeping that T-shirt you might be able to wear for one more day off the floor.'

Foundress Court at Pembroke College, Cambridge (ninety-six bedrooms), designed by Eric Parry Architects, and David Morley Architects' Maplethorpe Building for St Hugh's College, Oxford (also ninety-six bedrooms), followed, using variations on the basic designs.

LEFT The 'kit of parts' developed for study bedrooms and public spaces, originally for Newnham College but with variations to suit Pembroke, St Hugh's and subsequent projects. Storage dollies for the folding tables are included; open screens and open-ended hanging shelves maximize natural light in the bedrooms, while low tables have slatted shelves underneath to eliminate dust.

BELOW A suite composed of some of the elements shown in the illustration above. This is the Downing chair and St Hugh's desk, which went into Pembroke and St Hugh's. There are shorter and longer versions of the chaise longue.

RIGHT Conference pieces: the lectern continues the understated rectilinear aesthetic, matching the 'teaching' version of the folding table with its added modesty panels, making it useable in front of an audience.

ABOVE The Luke Hughes & Company lay figure trying out the various sitting and reclining positions available to him on the shorter version of the chaise longue (chaise courte?). 'Students don't sit in tub chairs; they just drape clothes over them,' says Luke, which is why the chaise longue form was chosen over the ubiquitous tub.

The chair, for example, was originally designed for Quinlan Terry's neo-classical Maitland Robinson Library at Downing College, Cambridge, but with each new accommodation project the design was tweaked to suit its context. 'The kit of parts was the same but we developed three different design languages,' says Luke. 'Those first three projects – Newnham, St Hugh's and Pembroke – were critical in developing our thinking, not just in how to make the furniture perform, but how to enable the building to perform better.'

Dining halls and meeting rooms provided Luke Hughes & Company with an opportunity to develop its range of reconfigurable and stackable tables and chairs. 'We looked for consistency right through the building, allowing the rooms to be used in different layouts. You can reconfigure a room with our folding tables – which don't look or feel like folding tables, thanks to the sophisticated engineering of the folding and locking mechanisms – from a temporary dining area to a ninety-six-seat dining hall to a space for a full-blown conference. Everything is modular so it all fits together in a minimum footprint for easy cleaning; low tables have magazine racks made of slats so they don't gather dust. Everything was thought through to minimize the colleges' maintenance bills.'

Luke ends the story by returning to 1990, when the whole process began. 'We pitched for the furniture for ninety-six bedrooms in a graduate block at Merton College, Oxford,' says Luke. 'The bursar said, "How much will it cost?" I said, "I don't know, we haven't designed it yet." "Give me a ballpark figure," he said. So I said, "One hundred and fifty to two hundred and fifty thousand pounds." He said, "Call it two hundred and fifty, but I don't want to spend more. The college last bought serious bedroom furniture in 1939 for the new Rose Lane buildings, and there have been no maintenance problems ever since. Do the same for me and I'm happy to spend the money now."

'"Brilliant!" I thought, and we got the job. The furniture has now been there for thirty years, with one breakage reported since 1990. I took one of our American dealers round recently, and John Gloag, the estates bursar, said, "It's absolutely true: there have been no maintenance problems in thirty years." I had to clench my fist and do a secret "Yessss!".'

ABOVE The finished article: an actual study bedroom at Pembroke College, featuring the later desk design with integral drawers.

BELOW, LEFT AND RIGHT Sketch drawing and photograph of the earlier desk design, as used at Newnham College. The effect is different from that of the later, squared-off designs for Pembroke and St Hugh's, relying on the curved-metal central bracing rod for the aesthetic. The wide overhangs of the top surface, for a pedestal unit below, are a feature of the 'kit of parts' approach, used in both desk designs.

RIGHT Top to bottom: Foundress Court, Pembroke College, Cambridge, by Eric Parry Architects; the Maplethorpe Building, St Hugh's College, Oxford, by David Morley Architects; and the Rosalind Franklin block for Newnham College, Cambridge, by Allies & Morrison, a contemporary comment on Basil Champneys's 1875 'domestic collegiate' version of the Queen Anne style.

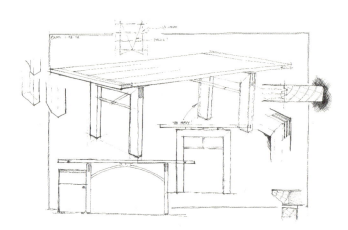

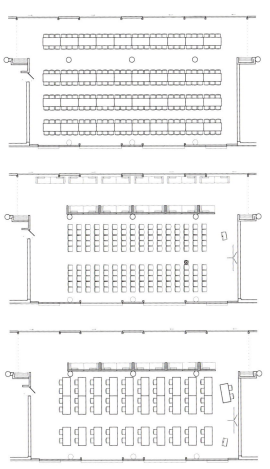

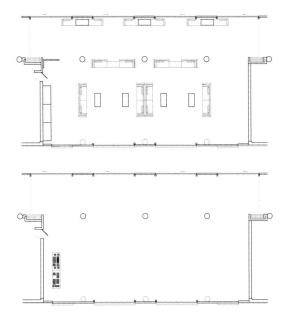

LEFT Space-planning variations for the multipurpose conference space at St Hugh's, showing a straightforward dining layout, a leisure option with sofas and chaises longues seen in the image below, an auditorium version with the maximum number of seats, a conference or lecture version with chairs and tables, and a clean sweep of empty floor.

BELOW The leisure and relaxation items from the 'kit of parts', as laid out in the conference centre at St Hugh's.

THE LEGGATE LECTURE THEATRE, UNIVERSITY OF LIVERPOOL

A tale of radial symmetry

'Alfred Waterhouse', says Luke, 'was one of those gutsy Victorian neo-Gothic architects doing lots of institutional and ecclesiastical work in the last quarter of the 19th century. Probably his most famous building is the Natural History Museum in London's museum quarter in South Kensington. Then there's St Paul's School; a series of buildings for Prudential Insurance, including the famous headquarters on High Holborn, London; many school and university buildings; and indeed – a building of sumptuous hideosity – the Victoria Building at Liverpool University.'

Luke is talking about the purpose-built headquarters for the university, which had occupied a disused lunatic asylum since its foundation in 1882, roughly contemporaneous with the crop of 'civic' universities founded in the late 19th century as institutions of practical and vocational education, in contrast with Oxford and Cambridge's classical and religious curricula. It is a magnificent neo-Gothic fantasy, replete with towers, gabled dormers and buttresses, expressed in Ruabon brick and terracotta dressings. Visitors familiar with the Natural History Museum's multi-material, exuberantly decorative forms will recognize the style in the Victoria Building, which, arguably, was the one from which the term 'red-brick university' was coined.

Funded largely by public subscription and private donations from the wealthy industrial and trading classes to whom Liverpool had been so kind in the 19th century, the building was opened in 1892, boasting – among many examples of Waterhouse's overheated

BELOW The University of Liverpool's red-brick Victoria Building by Alfred Waterhouse, one of the most confident of the Victorian neo-Gothic architects, well known for his idiosyncratic Natural History Museum in south-west London. The interior of the Leggate Lecture Theatre, as it was originally conceived and built, depended for its sweeping geometry on the magnificent skylight ceiling.

OPPOSITE The completed installation has an elegance that echoes Waterhouse's original vision for the space. Note the subtle, extra-width top rails of the chairs, a perfectly adequate resting place for notebooks and digital tablets.

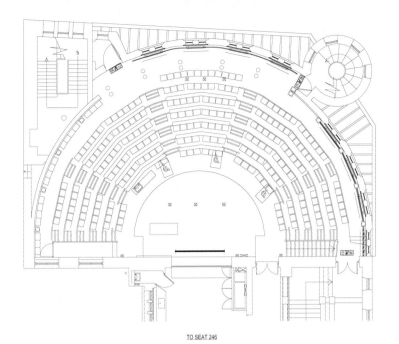

TO SEAT 246

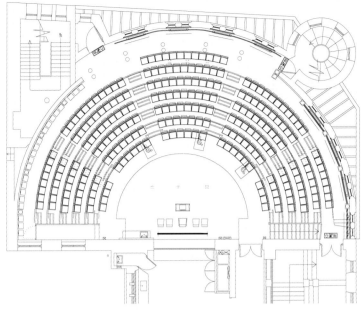

TO SEAT 260

ABOVE The plans for the raked seating show not only how much more visually pleasing the true semi-circular radius is than the straight-line-in-a-curve installation of the 1970s, but also that it accommodates fourteen more people. The heavy Columbian pine benches completely failed to live up to the driving radial idea of the design.

RIGHT This is (one of the places) where it got complicated. The vertical dimension between the rising platforms on which the chairs stand as they go up and back varies from platform to platform by as much as 40 millimetres (1½ in.). To comply with fire and health-and-safety regulations, the seat backs had to be a precise height and a precise horizontal distance from one row to the next. The enlarged top rail of each chair serves as a writing tablet.

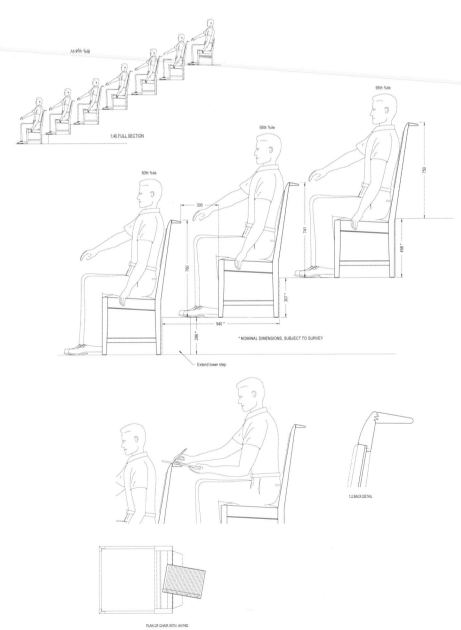

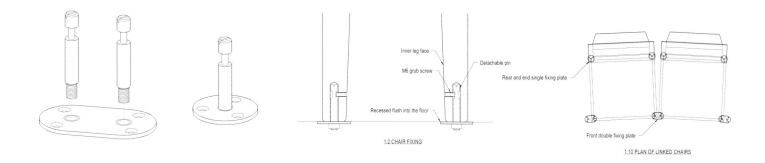

Inner leg face

M6 grub screw

Detachable pin

Rear and end single fixing plate

Recessed flush into the floor

1:2 CHAIR FIXING

Front double fixing plate

1:10 PLAN OF LINKED CHAIRS

ABOVE How the chairs, each one an independent unit, are held immovably together but on a radius that increases as you go up the levels, meaning that the front legs are touching while the back legs are further apart the further away from the centre they get. Plates let into the floor carry a sturdy, hardened steel pin with a machined neck, into which a grub screw locates through the side of the chair leg when the pin is sitting in its housing, drilled vertically into the underside of the chair foot. The plates carry two legs at the front but are separate at the back.

decorative imagination – the strictly functional yet supremely elegant steeply raked Leggate Lecture Theatre on the first floor.

'It's a particular kind of architectural type,' says Luke. 'It comes from the old medical-school model, where dissections and operations would be performed publicly, with all the medical students and a few ghouls and graverobbers craning their necks from the raked seats. It's all about sight lines.' The Leggate is by no means as spectacular as perhaps the UK's best example of such a space – the speech room at Harrow School – but the ceiling is nonetheless a thing of beauty, and the radially arranged seating round the performance and teaching area gives it its distinctive character.

But. 'In the 1970s,' continues Luke, 'someone from the Public Works Department had gutted the space because it didn't comply with the assorted regulations, and put in these lecture stalls in Columbian pine, which made no sense to the architectural interior whatsoever. They actually destroyed two things: the overall aesthetic effect, and the harmony of that radius, an incredibly important part of the architecture.

'The client said they only had £200 per seat to deal with the lecture seating. Levitt Bernstein, the architects doing the whole building's restoration, knew very well that integrated raked seating of the conventional theatre kind would be inappropriate, so the client asked, could we think of some way of dealing with that?

'I said, "This is such a good building, haven't you got anything from the archive of when it was built?" They said, "No, we haven't." I said, "Well, I've been to the RIBA Drawings Collection at the Victoria and Albert Museum, and this is what I found."' He is talking about a Waterhouse photograph that, says Luke, 'shows absolutely what the architect was trying to do. You can see the way the ceiling and the design of the chairs emphasize and enhance light and lightness. But the radius is very clearly expressed. It's absolutely fundamental.'

So the decision was made to go with separate chairs, which was where the technical complications started. 'We initially came up with the idea that the chair back would be the writing tablet – you only need about four inches – because we couldn't have standard writing tablets; they would have made it impossible to achieve

the necessary space between rows. But we had to work out a way of doing it because the rake of the platforms and the heights to which they rise all varied, as well, of course, as the radius increasing as you go outwards and upwards.'

The idea developed so that, as in the Queen's Building auditorium at Emmanuel College, Cambridge (page 158), the backs of the chairs in front and below became the handrail for the row behind and above, neatly complying with fire regulations. But to do that the chairs had to be permanently and securely fixed while still retaining their visual independence and allowing light to spread right across the room. Experiments with varying back heights to meet the changing measurements as the steps rise resulted in a two-height solution.

The fixing system, disarmingly simple in concept and solidly effective in use, keeps the chairs at exactly the same distance and angle throughout. A plate set into the floor carries an upstanding pin that locates in a hole bored into the endgrain bottom of the leg, and a grub screw inserted from the side of the leg fits into the thinner, turned neck-section of the pin. The plates for the front legs are double to carry neighbouring

chairs, and single for the rear legs, which have already splayed on the expanding radius. A desperately difficult thing to set out with pinpoint accuracy – a 1-millimetre discrepancy at one end of an eleven-chair row would result in a complete mis-fit at the other – the installation was a glowing testament to the combined skills of the Polish fitting team and the superbly accurate template work of Luke's design manager, Stephen Sharp.

'All this', says Luke, 'is about keeping site work down to a minimum and getting a chair to do more than one job: the seat, the tablet, the handrail. And we got fourteen more chairs in than with the ugly straight benches – and managed to retain and even emphasize Waterhouse's elegant radial design.'

There was a discussion about whether or not to upholster the chair backs. It was a popular idea, until it was realized how much natural light would be lost throughout the space. The decision was made, therefore, to go with slatted backs. 'But', says Luke, 'we found that the first versions, with only a few slats, allowed sight lines from the teaching area that, in the case of female students wearing skirts, might have proved compromising. So we added more slats – for the sake of propriety.'

YALE UNIVERSITY,
NEW HAVEN, CONNECTICUT

An architectural feast, and a variety of furniture-design responses

'Yale is frequently referred to as an outdoor museum of architecture,' wrote the then *New York Times* architecture critic Paul Goldberger, himself a Yale graduate, in a 1982 'walking tour' guide for the newspaper. 'The traveler passing through New Haven can see some of the best American architecture of the last hundred years in a single afternoon.

'The first and last important buildings in the career of Louis I. Kahn face each other across Chapel Street here, and they share the campus with major works by Eero Saarinen, Paul Rudolph, Philip Johnson and Edward Larrabee Barnes, among postwar architects, and James Gamble Rogers, John Russell Pope, and Carrere & Hastings among designers of an earlier generation.'

Writing in the early 1980s, Goldberger was of course well ahead of this century's most recent additions to the outdoor museum, two of which have presented Luke Hughes & Company with the kind of challenges that have given its 'furniture in architecture' philosophy increasing relevance and resilience. Working in leather and steel for Norman Foster's innovative School of Management, and overseeing a painstaking space-planning project for Robert A. M. Stern's Revivalist Benjamin Franklin College, could hardly be more different in project terms, but the same attitudes of

intelligent design and mature craftsmanship abide. The third job in this group – not counting the dining halls for the Yale–National University of Singapore collaboration (page 186), which stand apart – is actually two interiors in the Sterling Memorial Library, a mid-century Gothic behemoth with a distinct flavour of Giles Gilbert Scott's Cambridge University Library, England, designed and built at the same time.

The diversity of the architectural settings for Luke Hughes & Company at Yale might have given cause for a minor crisis of confidence in earlier years, but by the time these briefs arrived on the books in the second decade of the 21st century, the accumulation of thirty years of knowledge and experience was paying off. Not only had existing product designs gone through a range of developments and adaptations to suit numerous requirements, but also the by now substantial team's analysis of how a building is working and how it could be made to work better had reached a level of formal sophistication rare, if not unique, among craft-based furniture designers and makers on both sides of the Atlantic. There is perhaps an arguable sense in which the work at Yale University tells you all you need to know about Luke Hughes & Company.

OPPOSITE A taste of Yale's 'architectural feast' from the Hewitt Quadrangle. Located at the centre of the campus, the quadrangle is also known as Beinecke Plaza after the extraordinary Beinecke Rare Book and Manuscript Library, designed by Gordon Bunshaft of Skidmore, Owings & Merrill in 1963 with translucent marble panels in a brutalist granite façade. In the background is James Gamble Rogers's Lillian Goldman Law Library of 1931, modelled after King's College Chapel in Cambridge, England, in the 'collegiate Gothic' style.

EDWARD P. EVANS HALL,
YALE SCHOOL OF MANAGEMENT

Benchmarks for dramatic curves and powerful geometries

'The gist of this project was that we made friends with Yale,' says Luke. He is talking about the twenty-four curved, upholstered benches the company supplied at breakneck speed and well within budget for the new Edward P. Evans Hall, now the main building of the Yale School of Management. A massive 26,600 square metres (286,000 sq ft), the building is a signature piece by Foster + Partners, arranged over five floors around a central courtyard with distinctive, curving glazed façades and sixteen idiosyncratic, iridescent, double-height blue 'drums' housing the teaching and lecture rooms. 'Tailored to Yale's curriculum, the teaching spaces can support every style of learning,' say the architect's notes, 'from team-based working to lectures, discussions "in the round" and video conferencing.' On the principle that interaction outside the classroom is as important as formal teaching, the building has a variety of social spaces – a coffee shop, media library and large common room on the ground floor, and a wide internal circulation 'cloister'

on the second, the glazed façade mirroring the shapes of the blue drums to create areas where students can gather.

But spaces where students can gather need seating – which was a problem, as Yale's head of special projects, Mark Francis, explained to Luke in the back of a taxi on the way to Singapore airport. (They had both been in the country to discuss the furnishing of the dining halls at Yale-NUS College; see page 186.) Foster + Partners, whose eponymous principal had studied at Yale, had designed upholstered bench seating to fit the curved enclaves of its new building for the university, but Francis couldn't find a manufacturer in the US to make it for less than three times his budget. A twenty-minute taxi ride turned into an eighty-minute conversation, and Luke was on a plane again more or less as soon as he landed in London, his feet barely touching the ground. A strange twist that Luke Hughes's work for Yale in New Haven, Connecticut, would start the other side of the world in South East Asia.

BELOW The dramatic colonnaded exterior of the Edward P. Evans Hall, designed by Foster and Partners with an unusually exuberant combination of rectangular and circular forms. The five-story drums at the corners of this façade, with their distinctive rich blue cladding, are lecture halls; staircases are sandwiched in between

OPPOSITE Curved, leather-upholstered opposed-facing benches by Luke Hughes are designed as an architectural element in the 'Cloister' double-height circulation space on the second floor. It is intended for social interaction – hence the need for seating – and runs round the central open courtyard, the line of the wave form glazing determined by the circular lecture halls and echoed in the radii of the benches.

LEFT AND BELOW The robot that can compete with skilled and experienced upholsterers has yet to be invented, and remains a reassuringly long way off. The combination of manual skill and 'feel' for the material is paramount in the stitching of tough hide, with its elegant folded seams and drawn 'buttoned without the button' detail. The original plan was to use American hides, but time and cost considerations – the whole job of twenty-four enormous benches, from brief to delivery, had to be completed in nine weeks – rendered the idea unworkable. 'It was crazy to bring the hides over to England just to send them back again,' says Luke. 'Scottish leather does the job just as well.'

RIGHT Plan of the second-floor circulation space, showing the various circular or elliptical forms of the lecture halls and the positioning of the curved benches in the wave-form of the internal glazing. The school's administration services are housed in the rectilinear offices on the right; the horseshoe 'breakout' at the top is a dining hall; and the rectangle at the bottom, between the two staircases, is the library.

OVERLEAF Views of the benches, including a straight one, showing how they function not only as seating but also as foils to the architectural character of the space created by the curved glazing. They range in size from 6 to 7 metres (20 to 23 ft) in length, carry integrated power and data outlets, and locate over ventilation ducts. Truly furniture as architecture.

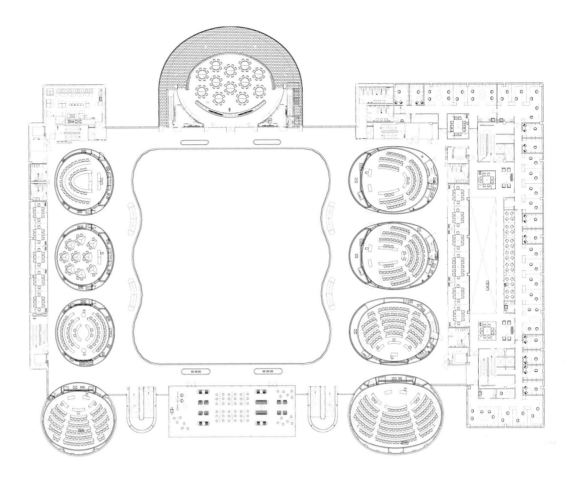

'The Foster concept was unmakeable for the money involved,' says Luke. 'We ended up taking it and making it happen for a fraction of the price they had been quoted by American manufacturers. There was also the problem of time. We had nine weeks before Bill and Hillary Clinton arrived to open the building in January 2014.'

Apart from producing drawings for rise-and-fall lecterns and lecture-theatre tables, the job was confined to twenty-four leather-upholstered benches, whose size, ranging from 6 to 7 metres (20 to 23 ft) in length, belies the word 'confined', and whose shape (except for the straight ones) follows the curves of the courtyard-facing glazing. 'Curves are difficult,' says Luke, 'especially on that scale.' Some of the pieces sport a central wedge-shaped back, allowing sitters to face either into the busy, animated interior or outward to the calm of the courtyard. They are 'cabled up', with integrated power and data outlets at accessible intervals, and designed to locate over floor-mounted ventilation ducts.

Leather and steel does not sound like a typical Arts and Crafts bill of materials, but the Victorians were no strangers to either. Luke Hughes & Company's production director, Nigel Shepherd, had extensive experience of leather upholstery from his time working for the likes of Aston Martin in the UK's automotive industry. 'Yale wanted us to use particular American hides,' says Luke, 'but I thought it was nuts to ship them over to England then ship them back again as part of a seat. We worked with Race Furniture in Bourton on the Water, Worcestershire, to make the upholstered parts.' All the steel structural components were laser-cut in Birmingham 'so that everything would slot together like origami', a requirement of the eye-wateringly tight schedule: contract, design, approval, manufacture, shipping, delivery and installation in nine weeks. There was no alternative, given the timing, to shipping the whole consignment by air, which meant flat-packing the components and assembling them on site.

'We got it there on time and on budget,' says Luke, 'and everyone was delighted.' Edward Snyder, the dean of Yale School of Management, is complimentary about the building as a whole and the benches in particular, which 'arouse a sense of interconnectedness, provide long lines of sight and encourage vibrant engagement'. The Luke Hughes team were perhaps more tickled to see one of their Yale benches in an IBM Watson ad with legendary but reluctant Nobel Laureate Bob Dylan, who picks up his Fender guitar and beats a hasty retreat when Watson, an artificially intelligent computer, breaks into song and starts 'Do-be-do-be-doo-ing' to the bard's departing back.

DINING HALLS, YALE-NUS COLLEGE, SINGAPORE

Furniture in architecture versus furniture by architects

Much more than designing furniture as product, this is a story of rigorous space planning and a furniture-design process driven by an intelligent understanding of how people behave in buildings, and of how furniture can optimize those buildings to support that behaviour. 'In our thirty-year experience,' says Luke, 'it's not just about product. It's about how you enable people to inhabit space elegantly and efficiently.'

Yale University's first-ever collegiate collaboration, with the National University of Singapore, is the first liberal-arts college in Singapore and one of the very few across Asia. It makes Yale the first Ivy League university to establish a college bearing its name in that part of the world. But the start of the project, at least, was

troubled. Singapore restricts freedom of assembly and association, and homosexual acts are illegal there. The response to this political environment – and to Yale's perceived subscription to it – from both Yale alumni and a good few other commentators and organizations was heated to say the least. 'Some of the strongest criticism has come from academics at Yale's campus in New Haven, Connecticut, as well as from rights groups,' wrote Liz Gooch in the *New York Times* on 27 August 2012. She quotes Phil Robertson, the deputy Asia director at Human Rights Watch: '"Yale is betraying the spirit of the university as a center of open debate and protest by giving away the rights of its students at its new Singapore campus."'

BELOW One of the three colleges on the campus. Pelli Clarke Pelli's well-mannered architectural response to typical Singapore style – sun- and rain-screened colonnades and generous overhanging eaves – works well in the context of the lush central courtyard garden.

OPPOSITE The dining hall of Saga College. The three dining halls furnished by Luke Hughes & Company are similar, but each has different roof and ceiling treatments. All the chairs used in the dining halls are the Luke Hughes Newnham model, but with variations in the back design to suit the specific interior. Such spaces are empty 80 per cent of the time, which means the 'rhythm of quantity' in the furniture must bespeak the room's function even when empty of people.

The presidents of the two institutions involved – Rick Levin at Yale, and Pericles Lewis at Yale-NUS – countered with the argument that one of America's most distinguished institutions of learning would expect to engage with such a social and political context, with a view to influencing it, and not remain aloof. Speaking at the groundbreaking ceremony on 6 July 2012, Lewis turned to the architecture to disarm the critics. 'The design of Yale-NUS College seeks to find an architecture which balances Eastern and Western contexts and traditions, but it has, in truth, created something new, something greater than the sum of its parts. Courtyards punctuated by towers set in lush landscapes, a close community of learning and social spaces, and a clear and inviting set of processional entrances matul la the openness, energy and optimism of the curriculum we are designing.'

'Pelli Clarke Pelli Architects certainly fulfilled their brief from Yale,' says Luke. 'Our job was to make the dining halls work.' He is very complimentary about César Pelli's practice, based in New Haven next to Yale University, and responsible for, among other massive corporate buildings, the 'mother ship' of Canary Wharf in London, One Canada Square. The architects of record, based in Singapore and dealing with local conditions and bureaucracy, were Forum Architects.

'We were originally on the pitch to look at all the furniture,' Luke says. 'We came up with a series of designs to try to reflect the Asian (and especially Chinese) feel of Singapore – endless permutations, including the bedroom furniture. We looked at different versions to make it work before the architects decided what they were going to do, playing all kinds of tunes on our normal stacking tables. The version we ended up

BELOW Space-planning drawing by Luke Hughes & Company, with Luke's handwritten note at top right: 'aligned on architectural features'. The geometrical process of lining everything up, and the mathematical one of calculating sizes and leg positions, are crucial to this kind of work. There are four layout options, one of which increases capacity by almost 25 per cent by using demountable tables.

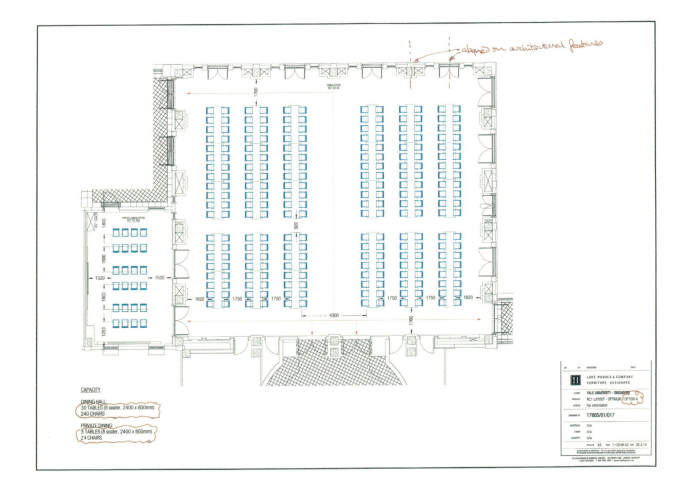

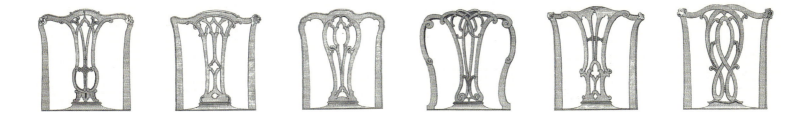

ABOVE Achieving a variety of chair designs just by changing the back on a standard model is not new, as shown by this drawing from Thomas Chippendale's *Gentleman and Cabinet-maker's Director* of 1754.

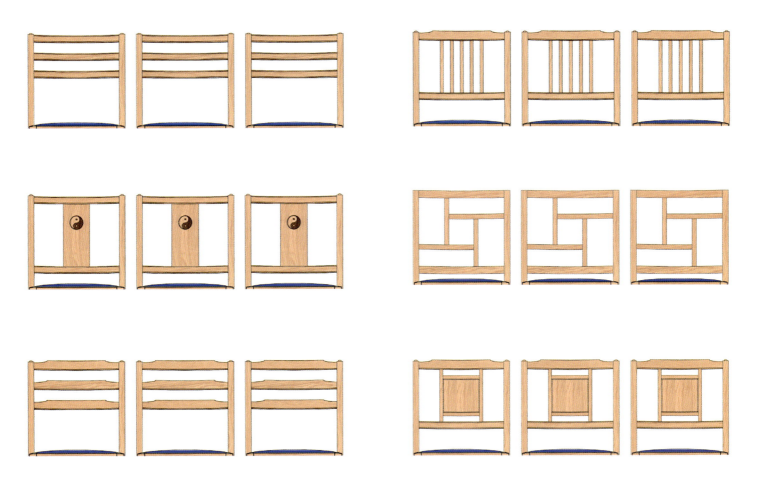

ABOVE Six chair-back designs proposed by Luke Hughes & Company for the three dining halls. The aim was to pursue the 'Chinese' aesthetic that the architect had adopted, best expressed in the bottom two options in the right-hand column.

with, a demountable table with a removable top and legs that can be stored separately, is actually the basis of the stuff we did for Keystone Academy in Beijing [page 222].'

The final contract did not include the bedroom furniture, but 500 chairs for each of three dining halls, plus both round and long tables, were certainly enough to be going on with. 'We used the structural frame of our basic Newnham chair, but with three different backs – an idea common to chair makers, like Thomas Chippendale, as long ago as the 18th century. Individually the chair frame is not particularly interesting, but the design becomes more vibrant and dominating when every little detail is multiplied by 500. That's one of the points about seeing chairs in quantity: you can no longer see them as individual pieces but only as part of a group. We worked closely with the architects to get the general rhythm of the whole thing, and we certainly got the dining halls working more effectively. Flexibility in the ways the furniture can be used was the main thing.'

Luke's enthusiasm for the architecture is tempered with evident frustration at the procurement route and the insistence of the architects at Forum on wanting 'to have a hand' in the design of the chairs. 'They kept redesigning the chair', he says, his patience clearly tried, 'to such an extent that I kept reflecting on what Sir Philip Dowson had confessed to me so many years before [see page 19].'

As far as the buildings themselves were concerned, continues Luke, 'sometimes you have to suspend your own taste, not out of pure commercialism, but because your end game is to make the building work. In fact, what we saw on the screen in front of us was actually not too bad in the context of the executed architecture.

For a restrained interior, an over-mannered chair with too much detail is not the answer. Vanity has to be suspended, and you still have to follow the principle: are you going to improve the architecture through enhanced functionality?'

Pelli Clarke Pelli had a clear idea of what they wanted to do with the joinery and how it would serve the overall concept – the windows, the roofscape, the flooring and the associated buildings. But the space planning was once again where Luke Hughes & Company were able to make a significant difference, and indeed to re-emphasize Luke's constant theme of furniture in architecture. 'When the layout drawings were sent through, we didn't think they worked. Nothing aligned. Here are the wall columns' – he points to one of the drawings – 'and the tables form no relationship to them. And no one seemed to have checked the positions of the table legs in relation to the chairs. It's maddening to have to straddle a table leg during a meal.

'We tidied it all up and increased the capacity – gave them lots of permutations. We aligned everything with the columns and architectural features, so it probably makes much more sense when you come into the space. We also engineered the tables down to a millimetre or two, so no one has to sit against a leg. The client and their students appear to be thrilled, and the project has led on to a close working relationship with Pelli Clark Pelli.'

INTERNATIONAL CONFERENCE ROOM AND MANUSCRIPTS AND ARCHIVES ROOM, STERLING MEMORIAL LIBRARY, YALE UNIVERSITY

Smart furniture for a library like a cathedral

Mark Francis, head of special projects at Yale, absorbing the glow from the palpable success and glamorous opening of the Edward P. Evans Hall of the School of Management by Bill and Hillary Clinton in January 2014, turned to the 'saviour of the benches' and said: 'And now, can you take a look at ...' He was pointing at the Sterling Memorial Library.

The Sterling is not quite Yale's architectural centrepiece – the Memorial Quadrangle by the same architect, with its 61-metre (200-ft) Perpendicular Gothic Harkness Tower owing much to England's 'Boston Stump', generally holds that title – but library and quadrangle together form the linchpin of the university's Gothic Revival campus. The Sterling resonates with Gothic cathedrals as much as Giles Gilbert Scott's Cambridge University Library does with his Battersea Power Station in London – perhaps more. Its architect, James Gamble Rogers, who took over the project from Bertram Goodhue on his death in 1924 through to completion in 1931, gave the building a cathedral plan 'as near to modern Gothic as we dared to make it' (quoted in Elizabeth Mills Brown, *A Guide to Architecture and Urban Design*, 1976).

At 11,380 square metres (122,500 sq ft) – which, when compared with the 26,600-square-metre (286,000-sq-ft) Edward P. Evans Hall, doesn't sound quite so massive – the building occupies more than half a city block and houses more than four million volumes. It also holds several special collections, including the university's Manuscripts and Archives Room. This is the storage, display and reference area to which Luke's attention was drawn, but only after – working with New Haven architectural practice Apicella + Bunton – he was charged with furnishing the newly commissioned International Conference Room. 'The librarians wanted a conference room cum flexible lecture space,' says Luke, 'for which our folding-table mechanism was perfectly suited.' The very plain and simple linoleum-topped tables, together with the leather-upholstered Luke Hughes Folio chair, provide a rectilinear counterpoint to the Gothic exuberance of the high – and highly decorated – vaulted ceiling and extravagantly moulded leaded-light windows. 'It was the usual approach,' says Luke, pointing out that the main design challenge for such a space was not so

BELOW The cathedral-like front façade of the Sterling Memorial Library – 'as near to modern Gothic as we dared to make it,' said its architect, James Gamble Rogers. The quasi-religious atmosphere is compounded by the figure of the medieval scholar over the doors, accompanied by inscriptions in Cro-Magnon, Egyptian, Babylonian and Hebrew.

OPPOSITE The 'Nave' entrance hall of the library, with its distinctive coffered ceiling, intricate leaded-light windows and linenfold panelling, all of which continue the decorative theme. The International Conference Room is off to the left, the Manuscripts and Archives Room to the right.

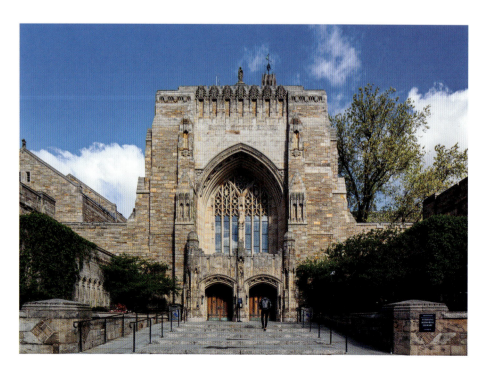

ABOVE The gloomy Manuscripts and Archives Room before the Luke Hughes and Apicella + Bunton makeover. The lighting, designed by the architects, did the whole space a huge favour, especially the Elizabethan 'homage' ceiling, whose carved and decorated beams now enjoy a direct relationship with the space.

OPPOSITE The main space of the Manuscripts and Archives Room, as seen from the mezzanine area through the decorative screen (top) and from the opposite end, looking up to the gallery and mezzanine, the handsome ceiling now visible. The technical complexity of the linoleum-topped tables is belied by their visual simplicity; the height-adjustable tops sit on hollow legs carrying data and power cabling to each of four users.

much furnishing it as storing the furniture when a clear floor was needed.

Hard on the heels of this comparatively small and unencumbered scheme was the Manuscripts and Archives Room, also known as the MSSA Room, in which it's easy to imagine generations of academics carefully poring over a variety of original documents relating to their chosen research project. As for 'encumbrance', this space represents the beating heart of the university, the place where the most precious pieces of its intellectual legacy reside, and in which the emotional attachment of those same generations of academics is cumulatively invested. For Luke Hughes & Company, again working with Apicella + Bunton, this was a job it had to get right.

'We used the same folding-table mechanism as we had in the conference room,' says Luke, 'and the Folio chair.' Table tops were finished in linoleum – another similarity to the conference room – to provide protective surfaces for the delicate documents. Static reception, librarians' and reference desks with cupboards behind all echo the handsome proto-Elizabethan panelling, which was restored and refurbished, along with the glass-fronted display cases. The gallery that runs round the main space culminates at one end in an ornately

carved and decorated screen, which encloses a further conference or meeting space with framed views to the ground floor below. 'The screen stayed,' says Luke, giving the merest hint of the lively discussions that had accompanied the development of the scheme amid the institutional (and predictable) instinct for preservation.

The real transformation for the MSSA – functional, elegant and efficient though the new furniture is – was in the lighting. 'It was pretty gloomy before work started,' opines Luke, with charming understatement. The hanging lamps, installed at a time when ambient lighting and the technology to achieve it unobtrusively were mere science fiction, contributed as much shadow as they did illumination, and could hardly be said to enable the room's main function: the reading of ancient, near-illegible manuscripts. With uplighters invisibly located along the tops of the upper tier of glazed and panelled bookcases, the whole space becomes a lively and welcoming one without losing its studious, academic seriousness. The warmth of the refurbished oak panelling animates the lower levels, while the proto-Elizabethan ceiling, with its carved and decorated beams, is shown to full advantage – as well as defining the elegant proportions of the room, whose height had been permanently lost in shadow.

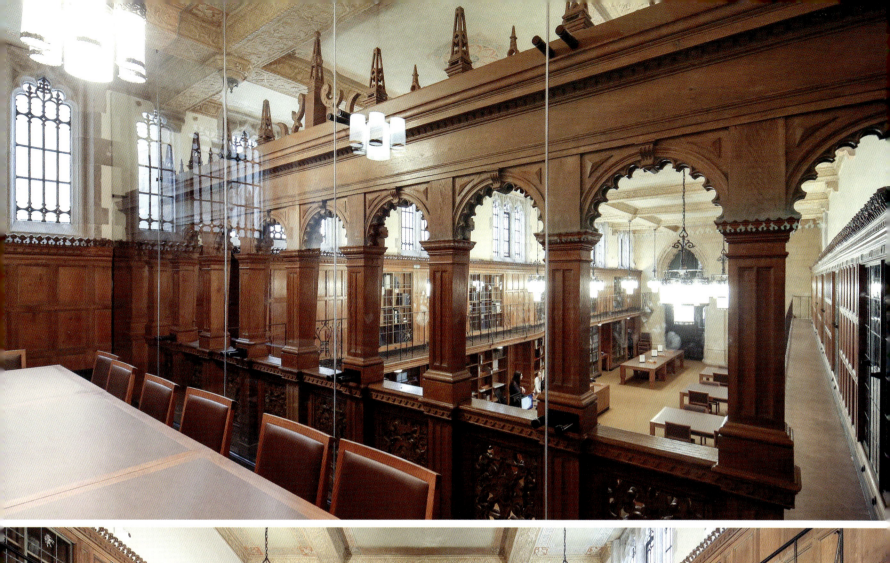

DINING HALL, BENJAMIN FRANKLIN COLLEGE, YALE UNIVERSITY

'Neo-neo Gothic' architecture furnished in 'slightly Tudor' style

'There is nothing wrong with copying history,' wrote Yale graduate and former *enfant terrible* of architectural criticism Aaron Betsky in the online *Architect Magazine* in May 2018. 'You just need a good reason and have to do it well.' He was introducing Robert A. M. Stern's eloquent exercise in reproduction neo-Gothic, one of two new Yale colleges opened for the 2017/18 academic year, for which Luke Hughes & Company designed dining-hall furniture, and by whose architecture Luke, for all his well-bred English politeness, is clearly a little challenged.

Stern, 'the reigning Prince of Corporate Classicism' according to Betsky, 'had a rationale to make the first new colleges Yale University built in half a century neo-Gothic: neither he, a graduate of the Yale School of Architecture, nor the client, nor the donors, nor (I imagine) the future student inhabitants could imagine anything else. Yale is neo-Gothic; that is its image and its "unique selling point."' Betsky also points

out that Stern, a personal friend, is the dean of Yale School of Architecture. 'Truth be told, it was inevitable that Dean Bob (he ran the School of Architecture for seventeen years until retiring in 2016) would get the job and turn to neo-Gothic. So, how has Stern done? Pretty well, all things considered. My judgment on this does not, however, mean that I either buy that it was the right thing to do or that the results are wholly successful.'

If each of the Luke Hughes & Company stories in this book is a story of responding to a building or buildings, it's evident that working with such a building as Stern's new college is a philosophical challenge that first-generation Arts and Crafts practitioners would not have had to confront, when the world was simpler and pastiche was yet to become familiar. 'We took the architectural concept', says Luke, speaking of the dining halls into which Luke Hughes & Company chairs and tables were to be installed, 'and turned it into something viable for furniture. The core story is to take

BELOW Robert A. M. Stern's neo-Gothic Benjamin Franklin College, opened in 2017, has a distinct flavour of Keble College, Oxford, or of Selwyn College in Cambridge. Yale's image is neo-Gothic, says critic Aaron Betsky. No one could imagine anything else.

OPPOSITE The dining hall, furnished with Luke Hughes & Company's suitably Gothic Wykeham chair, makes Luke's point about the 'rhythm of quantity' admirably. The tables do not fold, but some of them have removable tops with smaller ones underneath. This is one of four configurations, using smaller, round tables at each end of the space.

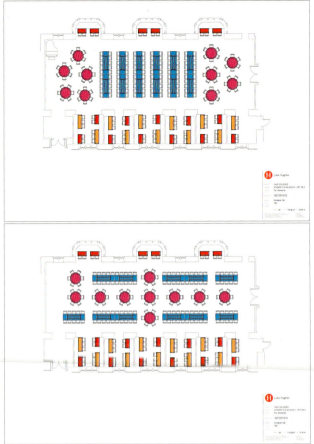

what the architect designed and respond appropriately. It's the same principle for dealing with very different architectural forms' – which Yale, of course, supplied. The job is always to make the building work better. 'In the case of Benjamin Franklin,' continues Luke, 'we ended up looking closely at the space planning and helping to make it far more efficient than had first been thought possible.'

With its triple-arched top rail, the Wykeham chair – a well-tried variation on a Luke Hughes & Company standard – was intended to have a slightly Gothic feel. It was therefore the obvious choice. 'Originally designed for New College, Oxford [page 236], it's actually quite a sophisticated chair,' says Luke. 'We used a stacking version at Benjamin Franklin. Like many other colleges in Oxbridge and the United States, they use their hall for a whole series of different types of dining, for plays, concerts and balls, you name it. We needed to achieve flexible space without compromising the building or breaking the backs of the people moving the stuff. Working on the layouts for the re-arrangeable tables, for instance, we collaborated closely with the catering team, looking at how they are really used.

'If the catering and facilities team can deliver a better service, then that's what we can do to help them.

We make furniture that's easier to handle and easier to store, without damage to the furniture itself or to the building. A year on and it's looking fantastic; it looks great in its setting.'

ABOVE Four alternative configurations showing the differently sized tops, all based on the same number of underframes. 'It shows how easy it is to reconfigure a space,' says Luke, 'once you get the sizes and the leg positions right.'

OPPOSITE Note, by comparing with the drawings above, how alignment of the elements with architectural features renders the whole space both manageable and visually coherent.

OVERLEAF Details of the chamfering on the Wykeham chair – 'a Gothic feel without a Gothic arch in sight,' says Luke, although the back does indeed suggest a Gothic arch. The modelling achieved by relieving the rectangular components of their hard edges adds to the play of light and shadow, and articulates the rhythm of quantity mentioned earlier.

SAINSBURY LABORATORY, UNIVERSITY OF CAMBRIDGE

World-class science, world-class architecture, world-class furniture

OPPOSITE The particular genius of architects Stanton Williams, Modernists to a fault, was to imbue a potentially stark linear and planar concept with harmony and warmth by means of meticulous attention to space, proportion and detail. Materials are not confined to exclusively 'natural' ones – unless steel and concrete can be considered natural – but, in a contemporary take on the Arts and Crafts philosophy, they are honest and honestly presented, which gives the building its humanity.

BELOW Geometric precision, elegant linear proportions, the warmth of natural oak and finely engineered 'shadow gaps' characterize the furniture throughout the building.

The Cambridge University Botanic Garden was the brainchild of John Stevens Henslow, professor of botany at the university from 1825 until his death in 1861, and the loved and revered mentor of Charles Darwin. Henslow's research focused on the nature and origin of species, and his influence and inspiration are much credited in Darwin's revolutionary work. Founded in 1846, the garden is home to 8,000 plant species, including an array of trees that form one of the UK's finest arboretums.

In the first years of the 21st century, against a background of a burgeoning world population and a consequent, urgent need for agricultural innovation, it became apparent that the university required a world-class post-doctorate facility for its Botanic Institute. The laboratory should attract the very best scientists, and would cement the university's reputation for the most advanced botanical research on the planet.

Lord Sainsbury of Turville, in line for election as the next chancellor of the university after Prince Philip's retirement, was keen to fund the project through his Gatsby Charitable Foundation. Architects Stanton Williams were appointed to design what had to be a signature building in every respect. 'One of the ways that Stanton Williams really distinguished themselves', says Roger Freedman, the foundation's chief scientific advisor to the Sainsbury Laboratory, 'was that they dedicated quite a long time to understanding what their remit was, what the building had to be. And they also took time to look at the site. And when they had digested those issues, that was when they started sketching out general ideas. They really listened.'

One of Stanton Williams' characteristic attitudes to design, in order to guarantee aesthetic coherence throughout a project, is that they must have control of every last detail. When the subject of furniture arose

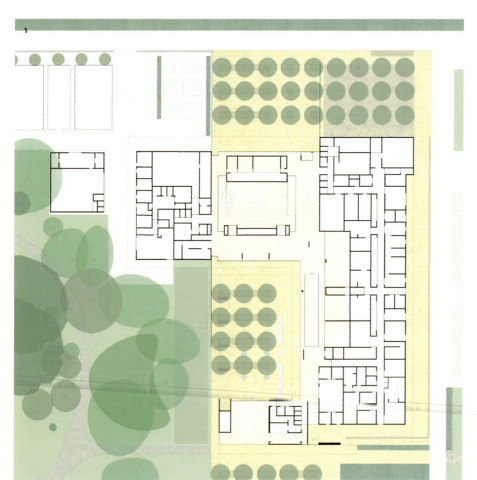

The architects' plan and visual renders show how the building addresses its natural surroundings, extending the 'open space' feel of the fully glazed interior through the courtyard and open terraces to the garden and arboretum. Perhaps the most dramatic view of the building (bottom), which will be partially obscured as the planting matures, reveals the subtle rhythm and graceful proportions of the rectilinear volumes. 'The building's identity is established externally by the way in which it is expressed and experienced as a series of interlinked yet distinct volumes of differing height grouped around three sides of a central courtyard,' say the architects. The café with its outside tables provides the animated link between laboratory and garden.

RIGHT Detail drawing of the development of the characteristic shadow gap that occurs throughout the furniture suite – and indeed throughout the building. The dimensioned drawing has been scribbled on during a meeting to discuss the addition of a 5-millimetre ($^1/_4$-in.) spacer between frame and oak top; 'Agreed with Stanton Williams' is the note in Luke's handwriting.

FAR RIGHT Craftsman Joe Latta milling a steel table component at A. Edmonds & Co., the metalworkers' workshop in Birmingham that undertook such challenging work for the project. Just because it's metal doesn't mean there's no craftsmanship involved; in fact, as we saw in 'A Tale of Two Tables' (page 124), it is craftsmanship that gives stainless steel its machine aesthetic.

– very early on in the project, since Stanton Williams rarely consider the interiors as separate from the architecture – Lord Sainsbury recommended Luke Hughes, who had recently designed and made his dining table: 'The only person we know with a similar approach to yours when it comes to detail.'

From the moment of the subsequent call from Stanton Williams founding partner Alan Stanton, says Luke, it became a 'hugely enjoyable' eighteen months to two years. It was as if the Luke Hughes & Company philosophy – that in any quality building, the connection between the architecture and the furniture should be seamless – had been given the perfect opportunity to demonstrate its fundamental truth. A schedule of all the furniture types the building needed – soft public seating, low tables, desks, research pods, study bedrooms, credenzas, carrels, meeting and conference tables – was drawn up and priced at low and high points to meet the budget. 'Which was very tight,' says Luke. 'Our job was to find a clever way of procuring the furniture to stay on budget but not diminish the architecture in any way. The budget is a design criterion, one of the things that we can get some engineering into. There's no point in designing something then discovering the client doesn't have the money.'

Alan Stanton worked closely with the Luke Hughes team throughout the project, considering every detail and contributing to the design language that evolved, in material terms, into leather upholstery in a shade of pewter – to match the building's structural columns – oak and stainless steel. 'There were a lot of meetings and a lot of models,' says Luke. 'We kept going back to the building to try to understand it better. And we took Alan to the workshops to look at stainless-steel welding, to the upholsterers to test the "give" in the dual foam layers, to decide on cricket-ball seams or pleated ones,

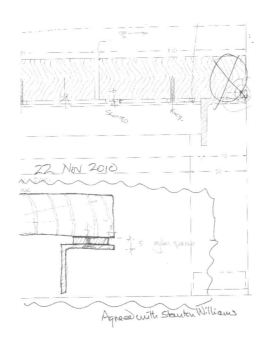

to control the stretching and stitching so the leather didn't crease or ruck up.'

The steel presented a number of making challenges as the pieces developed, carrying the shadow-gap detail evident everywhere in the building. 'We didn't know how we would make the steel components when we started,' explains Luke. 'Stainless steel is much more ductile than mild steel, so when you weld it the heat can distort it.' Where the welds went and what happened in the process was a matter of trial and error, driving the decisions about folding or joining the material and a host of other issues. 'We were drawing as we were making,' continues Luke. 'How far could we make those shadow gaps work? Then some of the tables are two and a half metres [8 ft] long, with no triangulation at the corners for strength or rigidity. The whole thing depends entirely on the strength of the steel itself.'

The Sainsbury Laboratory was opened by the Queen in April 2011. The profound commitment to quality and painstaking attention to detail is everywhere apparent, in the 'soft' human issues of circulation, co-operation and collaboration, as well as sustainability and fitness for purpose, in an envelope of calm, restrained beauty. And, as if to purposely emphasize the Luke Hughes philosophy, the furniture's relationship to the building is indeed seamless. 'The palette of natural materials ... which includes powder-coated and anodised aluminium, stainless steel and acoustic render, is held together by impeccable detailed design,' wrote the critic Felix Mara in the *Architects' Journal*.

The project has received no less than thirteen awards and commendations – including, in 2012, the Stirling Prize, British architecture's highest accolade. (A later readers' poll in the *Architects' Journal* voted the building the best of all the previous Stirling Prize winners.) 'The

BELOW A schedule of all the furniture types the building needed – soft public seating, custom occasional tables, workstations, research pods, credenzas, carrels, custom meeting and thirty-seat conference tables – was drawn up to meet the 'very tight' budget, but not diminish the architecture in any way.

OPPOSITE The stainless steel presented a number of making challenges, carrying the shadow-gap detail evident everywhere in the building. It was to a large extent experimentation, seeking a process by which the steel components could be easily made. Where the welds went and what happened drove decisions about folding or joining and a host of other issues.

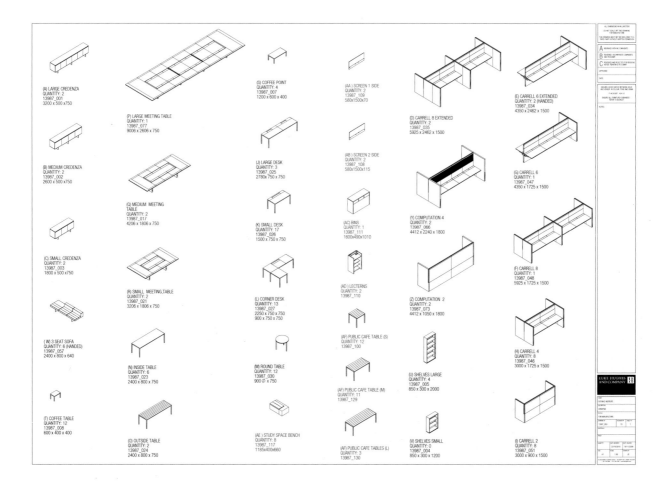

PREVIOUS PAGES Clockwise from top left: workstation carrels set out on the upper floor, with low tables and soft seating by Dynamobel. The colour of the leather upholstery was specified to match the powder-coated columns as closely as possible. The refectory and lecture theatre, with lecterns faced with brushed steel, maintain the atmosphere of calm concentration.

OPPOSITE A finishing detail of the cable-management flap in an oak desktop demonstrates the precision of the craftsmanship throughout the building.

ABOVE A conference table for thirty people presented its own challenges when it came to making the ubiquitous shadow gap work. The cellular office desk and round table show how well the design idea suits different forms; some of the tables are 2.4 metres (8 ft) long, with no triangulation at the corners for strength or rigidity. The whole structure depends entirely on the strength of the steel itself, the construction method and the quality of the jointing.

OVERLEAF Left: the interior's spectacularly successful relationship with the external world constantly refers to the building's ambition to become a world-class centre of excellence in plant science. Right: a detail of a writing shelf above the upholstered seating, should inspiration occur during repose.

Sainsbury Laboratory is a timeless piece of architecture,' said the judges, 'sitting within a highly sensitive site, one overlooking the woods where Darwin walked with his tutor and mentor Henslow, discussing the origin of species. In this project Stanton Williams and their landscape architects have created a new landscape, a courtyard which flows out into the botanical gardens. The project is both highly particular and specialised, and at the same time a universal building type, taken to an extraordinary degree of sophistication and beauty.'

'This is one of the most exciting projects with which my charitable foundation has been involved,' said Lord Sainsbury at the opening. 'It combines an inspirational research programme, an historic site in the Botanic Garden and a beautiful laboratory designed by Stanton Williams, and I believe it will become a world-class centre of excellence in plant science.'

'It was clear from the outset', concludes Luke Hughes, 'that Lord Sainsbury wanted an outstanding building. That is exactly what he got, and we are delighted to have been part of the project.'

SAINSBURY WELLCOME CENTRE FOR NEURAL CIRCUITS AND BEHAVIOUR, UNIVERSITY OF LONDON

Furniture for neuroscientists

'There's nothing in this job that's like pretty much anything else we have done,' says Luke. 'Not a stick of "real wood" to be seen, apart from a bit of veneered ply.' He is talking about the building known as the Sainsbury Wellcome Centre, the state-of-the-art neuroscience research centre for the University of London, and winner of numerous awards for its architect, Ian Ritchie.

Standing on a busy inner-city street near the main university site, the building's innovative approach to lab design is based on the idea that interaction between theoretical and experimental scientists – from many countries and with a wide range of specialities and knowledge – is key to fostering the sort of collaboration on which scientific breakthroughs depend. Ritchie's furniture brief to Luke Hughes & Company enshrines the same idea: ease of communication between colleagues, but with enough privacy to support sustained concentration. 'Maximum freedom for the science to flourish,' in the architect's own words.

Similarly, explains the architect, the building's interior 'is organized in accordance with neuroscientific research indicating a human preference for designed spaces with high visibility and connectivity, with multiple vantage points, various visual volumes and permeability. This multi-scale approach reflects the "scale-free network" of the brain.'

Tables for classrooms and cafés, lecterns, shelving systems and soft furniture for public areas were all on the specification list. 'We designed the tables with lightweight, polyurethane foam-injected edges and folding legs,' says Luke. 'The detailing is very crisp, like the overall look and feel of the building. There's a lot of flexibility for various different uses, and some of the tables were specific to narrow spaces.' The distinctive undulating front façade of the building is picked up in the shape of the table tops in the areas for social interaction, such as the terraces.

BELOW The wave form of the translucent glazed exterior of the building is picked up throughout the interior and in the furniture. The steel 'pixels' hanging from the soffit of the pedestrian-friendly colonnade show on one side portraits of the University of London's Noble laureates in physiology or medicine, and, on the other, the entire musical *oeuvre* of Johann Sebastian Bach in the form of sheet music.

OPPOSITE The 120-degree carrels, here laid out in line rather than a cluster. The job, says Luke, demanded engagement on multiple levels: 'How to synthesize all the things Ian Ritchie knows as an architect, how to get our own brains in gear to synthesize everything we know, and then make something better than everyone expected. That's the joy of it.'

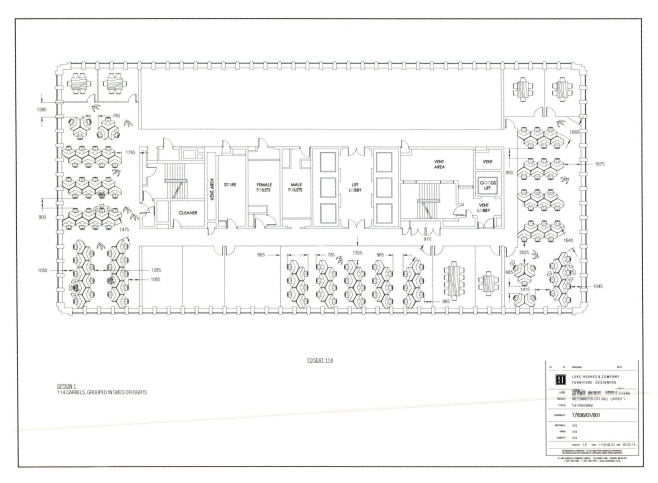

TO SEAT 114

OPTION 1
114 CARRELS, GROUPED IN SIXES OR EIGHTS

LUKE HUGHES & COMPANY
FURNITURE DESIGNERS

WESTMINSTER CITY HALL - LAYOUT 1

17836/01/001

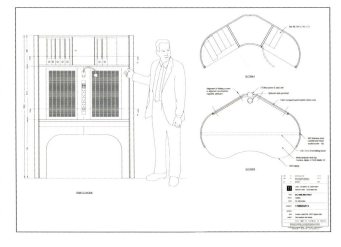

ABOVE, TOP Space planning was key to the project's success. This layout, actually prepared for Westminster City Hall in London, shows the variety of ways in which the 120-degree carrels can be configured, allowing a far higher density than in standard open-plan offices but keeping the humanity of the space.

ABOVE, LEFT, AND LEFT, BOTTOM A render and model of the carrel design in its original clover-leaf concept. The need to combine privacy with the ability to converse with one's colleagues was a crucial component of the brief.

ABOVE Construction drawings showing the main laminated ply 'walls' from which everything else is hung. Their size was a challenge, pushing Luke's knowledge of laminating to its limits. Acoustic wadding is laid into the fabric-wrapped vertical panels immediately in front of the occupant.

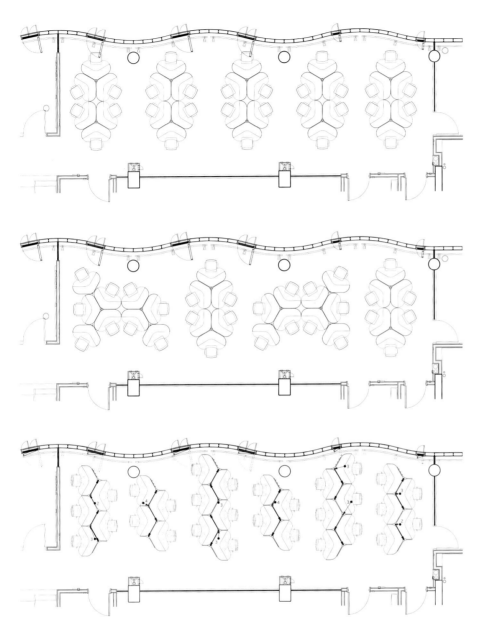

'The crucial thing, however,' says Luke, 'was the carrels. We were trying to do something completely different from open-plan office desking, to come up with a way of maintaining privacy while keeping the banter alive. They have acoustic wadding behind the pinboards, integral lighting and power – all the services. We only had about £750 per space, so the budget, as well as the footprint, was very tight.'

The real key to the success of the project was the space planning. Luke Hughes & Company's 120-degree format for the workstation carrels, continues Luke, 'enabled us to pack in a hell of a lot of people, far more than you would in open plan. The acoustic screening meant the units had to be high, which also gives that privacy, but flexibility and manoeuvrability were major parts of the brief, and the 120-degree configuration solved all those issues. The units were easy – and incredibly cheap – to make, and stacked very efficiently in a container.' The moulded and laminated ply shells were made in Slovenia, but their size was a challenge in terms of accuracy. '[I] had no fear of doing it,' says Luke, 'because this is what I learnt at a very early age in Mike Johnson's harpsichord workshop when I was still at school.'

ABOVE Three layout variations, the top two following the original 120-degree concept, which allows more room between clusters and creates a little more personal space. The bottom configuration was the one eventually chosen.

OVERLEAF The design follows 'a human preference for designed spaces with a multi-scale approach [that] reflects the "scale-free network" of the brain'.

OPPOSITE The curvatures created as a result of size and geometry also happen to make for an ergonomically sound workstation. (The books are screen-printed; there is no magical, extra depth for them.) The wave theme persists in the reception benches, the tables on the roof terrace, and elsewhere.

BELOW Shelving on the flat walls for the 'standard' workstations is a combination of proprietary track and specially designed brackets. The straightforward tables without the wave form are very light but very tough, the polyurethane-injected edges to the foam-core tops giving them a crisp linearity.

The themes of the project from Luke's point of view were the materials – a complete departure from the familiarity of solid timber – the innovative space planning, and the fruitful and creative relationship with the architect. 'I've worked with Ian on six separate projects,' says Luke. 'He has confidence in us. It was an incredibly tight manufacturing brief, an incredibly tight footprint, and a very demanding architect who knows how to achieve incredibly high standards.

'Although there's very little in the building that is like anything else we've done, the intellectual approach was the same. It's about making the building work. Using technology and materials in a clever way, drawing on knowledge gained from an entirely different source – it all came together in a way you would never have expected without a really good client and a really good architect. This is what I enjoy with these problems. We haven't got the money, so we have to use our brains – how to synthesize all the things Ian knows as an architect, how to get our own brains in gear to synthesize everything we know, and then make something better than everyone expected. That's the joy of it.'

KEYSTONE ACADEMY LIBRARY, BEIJING

Literature, language and East–West cultural exchange

Around the turn of the century, Luke Hughes committed himself and his company to respond, in the language of craft and design, not only to the architectural but also to the cultural traditions at work in such diverse buildings as Westminster Abbey in London (page 32) and Ahrends, Burton & Koralek's quirky British Embassy in Moscow (page 118). It is from this period that his conviction about the place of furniture in architecture became the heart of his business plan.

As a project, the High School Library of Keystone Academy, Beijing, offered an arguably richer level of cultural engagement, neatly capturing the persistent 'East meets West' conundrum as a direct theme for the design. Founded in 2014, and led by its visionary principal, Malcolm McKenzie, Keystone sees itself as a world school founded on three keystones: bilingual immersion in Chinese and English; building character and community throughout a residential setting; and promoting Chinese culture and identity in a world context.

But the academy was not housed in a building of merit, not by any means. The rash of cheaply made, off-the-peg skyscrapers spreading across the urban backlands of China's astonishingly fast-growing cities had not missed the area where Keystone is located. For Luke, the story was all about the interior, where there was more a less a clean slate – plus an unprecedentedly rich, inspirational palette of myth, magic and humanity's entire legacy of letters.

'In early meetings I was impressed by the books in the office of Song Jingming [the academy's director of libraries],' says Luke. 'From Kahlil Gibran to Thoreau's *Walden* in Mandarin, Robert Frost next to *Tao Te Ching*, patterns of porcelain and three hundred Tang poems. She seemed so engaged, so stimulating about Chinese culture, and equally absorbed by English literature, or rather literature in the English language – what it meant and what it might mean.' The potential of the project filled Luke, himself an embryonic Oriental

BELOW The everyday exterior of the building that houses the academy, one of the many behemoths demonstrating the relentless pace of China's urbanization. The interior is a different matter.

OPPOSITE The dramatic 'Moon Door' entrance to the library, complete with dancing-dragon door handles: 'The moment when a student physically grabs hold of the sense of these cultural connections.'

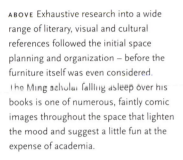

ABOVE Exhaustive research into a wide range of literary, visual and cultural references followed the initial space planning and organization – before the furniture itself was even considered. The Ming scholar falling asleep over his books is one of numerous, faintly comic images throughout the space that lighten the mood and suggest a little fun at the expense of academia.

ABOVE AND BELOW Colour is immensely significant in Chinese tradition, each 'standard' hue having a direct relationship to one of the five elements. The most auspicious were chosen to demarcate the different zones of the library: quiet or group study, offices, Scholars' Room, rare books. The red of the temple door (above) is one such hue, standing for the element of fire, and symbolizing happiness, luck, joy, vitality and celebration. It also acts as a guard against evil. The yellow of the Song-dynasty vase (below) is for the element Earth; beautiful and prestigious, it is an imperial colour representing power, royalty and prosperity. The Qing-dynasty vase (below, left) is decorated in a cobalt blue common to Chinese ceramics from the Ming dynasty onwards, signifying health, prosperity and harmony.

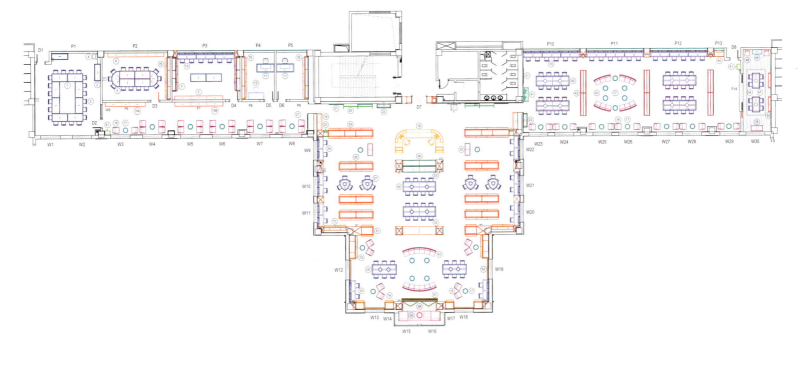

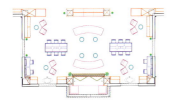 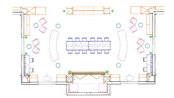 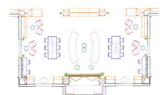 

ABOVE The library is designed around a central circulation area that includes wings for quiet and group study, teaching rooms, the librarians' office and the Scholars' Room, which contains rare and historic books. The entire space is furnished for flexible layouts so that zones can be used for different functions: lectures, poetry readings, concerts.

OVERLEAF The view towards the Moon Door from behind the reception desk. Folio chairs and new 'Keystone tables' give a contemporary twist to Ming- and Song-dynasty furniture forms.

scholar, with his customary enthusiasm: 'I understood what they were trying to do, and I knew I really wanted the job.'

The brief was to create a space that was a blend of Eastern and Western aesthetics and sensibilities, but reflecting the 21st-century world of digital communication and the notion of unlimited access to unlimited information. As the project evolved, it became an important part of the brief to convey the values of European and American libraries as they'd developed over the last millennium, while projecting the ethos of Keystone as a Chinese institution with an international flavour. Finding a starting point amid this complexity was a challenge, but a welcome one. 'How would we translate it into a 21st-century academic institution with relevance to Oxford, Cambridge, Yale, Harvard and the rest of them?' asks Luke.

Before the furniture, there was the research, and indeed the task of making the unprepossessing basic interior itself a suitable blank canvas. 'We worked it up looking at the layouts first of all – trying to make sense of the space even before we started on the style. How it could be flexible, how the lighting would work, how we would create spaces away from the sun. I began looking at Chinese references: an exhibition of marvellous silk

paintings at the Victoria and Albert Museum, an old Ming-dynasty scholar falling asleep over his books – a whole range of elements and images. We didn't want to be slavish, but I did want to learn from the visual references.'

The interior space was transformed through the use of colour. 'I thought the simplest thing we could do is paint it with traditional Chinese colours,' says Luke, 'and use colour as a device to differentiate the different zones.' The yellow glaze of a Song-dynasty vase is considered in Chinese tradition as the most beautiful and prestigious colour, signifying neutrality and good luck, while the deep rich red of the 'Moon Door' surrounds, which carries through the whole library, is also the colour of good fortune and joy.

The furniture schedule included oak reading tables and lecterns, leather-upholstered seating, and oak bookshelves and storage units. 'We consciously took some of the furniture forms illustrated in silk paintings from the Ming and Song dynasties and gave them a contemporary twist,' says Luke. But the project needed more than just furniture to create a vital academic environment, and is rich with a range of decorative ideas that demonstrate the depth of Luke Hughes & Company's experience with libraries. 'Artworks

are absolutely fundamental,' continues Luke. 'There were these wretched columns all over the place, so I decided to make a virtue of them. We commissioned the letter-carver Caroline Webb to do the letter-cutting of quotes and aphorisms into slate, and Dong Han, the calligraphy teacher at the academy, provided beautiful ink-brush lettering in Mandarin. We collected antiques from Beijing architectural salvage yards, and covered the columns with twenty-four long, narrow pictures of libraries and literary icons from round the world and throughout history. There's the British Museum from the time when Marx was writing *Das Kapital* there; the Strahov Library in Prague, because that is the main Jesuit library, and the Jesuits were the main link between China and the West from 1595 onwards; and even the Rosetta Stone.'

The *pièce de résistance*, in Luke's estimation, is the double-dragon door handles on the library entrance – 'the moment when a student physically grabs hold of the sense of these cultural connections' – inspired by an idea by Song Jingming. Commissioned from Scottish sculptor Jill Watson, the dragons themselves were the result of painstaking research. 'We must have photographed three hundred dragons,' says Luke. In the final installation, both Welsh and Chinese versions of the mythical animal breathe fire at each other across the doorway, embodying the act of communication that lies at the heart of academic learning.

The preliminary interior design in place, Luke Hughes & Company found itself with four months to design, manufacture, deliver and install 24 tonnes of furniture to a destination the other side of the world. Such a schedule stretched the firm's planning and logistical experience to the limit. 'We have put a lot of co-ordination techniques in place over the years,' says Luke. 'We used every single one of our sixteen workshops, plus some in Spain and Slovenia. Every single stick of the 24 tonnes had to be designed to go into the lifts – no one was going to be carrying all that furniture up the four flights of stairs.' The project, five container loads carefully packed in the correct installation sequence, was delivered ahead of time and under budget.

THIS PAGE The whole interior was furnished with paintings, art and sculpture – traditional and modern, Western and Eastern – to express the bibliophilic atmosphere. The columns became perfect grounds on which to hang images of libraries from all over the world and throughout time, including the British Museum Reading Room in the 1850s, when Karl Marx was writing *Das Kapital* there, and the Theological Hall in Strahov Abbey, Prague – 'because it's the main Jesuit library, and the Jesuits were the main link between China and the West from 1595 onwards'.

1 Books from the chained library (*c.* 1680) at Wells Cathedral, England.
2 Detail from a copy of the *Diamond Sutra*, one of the earliest examples of a dated woodblock-printed book (*c.* 900), found in Dunhuang, Western China.
3 Daoist gods, used as the cover illustration for one of the volumes in Joseph Needham's monumental series 'Science and Civilisation of China'. Needham chose the image to serve as a metaphor for the way China and its scientific and technical traditions had been viewed by the West.
4 'Three Laughs at Tiger Brook' shows Confucius presenting the young Gautama Buddha to Laozi – a fictional meeting but one continuously depicted in literature and various art forms as a representation of tolerance, inclusiveness and the convergence of the main philosophies in China.
5 Ma Gong Ding, the famous bronze tripod vessel from the Western Zhou dynasty (1100–771 BC), now in the Palace Museum in Taipei City.
6 Shiba Ryotaoro Museum (2001), Osaka, Japan.
7 Bibliothèque Sainte-Geneviève (1850), the public and university library in Paris, renowned as 'a temple of knowledge and space for contemplation'.
8 Detail from 'Prosperous Suzhou' (1759), a silk handscroll commissioned in 1751 by the Qianlong Emperor, showing the site of Suzhou government decorated with red silk and calligraphy banners in anticipation of civil-service examinations.

9 Detail of the Rosetta Stone (196 BC) showing the same inscription in the scripts of ancient Greek, cuneiform (used in Mesopotamia from the 34th century BC) and Egyptian hieroglyphs (developed in the 32nd century BC).
10 St Jerome (*c.* 347–420), the priest, theologian and historian best known for his translation of most of the Bible into Latin.
11 Xuanzang (*c.* 602–664), a Chinese Buddhist monk, scholar, traveller and translator, famous for his journey to India to receive instruction and obtain accurate Buddhist texts. He first translated more than six hundred texts from Sanskrit, thus forming the basis of all later Buddhist commentaries across China, Japan and Korea.
12 The Jesuit library in the Theological Hall (1679) of the Strahov Abbey in Prague, Czech Republic, the principal repository of the written reports about China that began to trickle to Europe from the 16th century onwards.
13 Detail of the frontispiece (and one of the earliest Western representations of Confucius) from the collection of various Jesuit reports about China and its neighbours (1735), collated by Father Jean-Baptiste Du Halde.
14 An 1857 photograph of the British Library Reading Room, where Karl Marx wrote *Das Kapital* almost contemporaneously with this early depiction of the interior.

OPPOSITE The long internal windows that separate the corridors from study areas were a problem; it was essential to bring light deep into the floorplate but without it being overlooked. The solution was a collection of aphorisms and quotations from the world of reading, books and libraries, carefully selected so they appear in Chinese, Latin and English, designed by Brian Webb and printed as a tint on translucent film that was then applied to the windows. Luke's favourite? Groucho Marx on the book as man's best friend, 'outside of a dog. Inside of a dog, it's too dark to read.'

That perfect tranquillity of life, which is nowhere to be found but in retreat, a faithful friend and a good library.
APHRA BEHN

THEY WHO KNOW THE TRUTH ARE
知之者不如
NOT EQUAL TO THOSE WHO LOVE IT,
好之者,好之
AND THEY WHO LOVE IT ARE NOT EQUAL
者不如乐之者 孔子
TO THOSE WHO DELIGHT IN IT.

We have preserved
the book,
and the book
has preserved us.
JEWISH QUOTATION

Within libraries
what have we?
We have no past
and no future.
RAY BRADBURY

It is what you read when you don't have to that
determines what you will be when you can't help it.
OSCAR WILDE

'There was a great joy about the whole project,' says Luke, for whom it represented considerable personal and professional advances. The client and the users, especially the students, were nothing short of ecstatic. Song Jingming's comment perfectly expresses the genuine delight of both staff and students: 'Places where the *qi* (energy) not only draws you in but also speaks of other eras (and values) are so rare. The Jin-dynasty poet Tao Yuanming wrote in "The Peach Blossom Land" about a fisherman who stumbled on a magical village where, on entering, visitors lose their sense of time and forget to leave. That is what the library feels like.'

PREVIOUS PAGES Clockwise from top left: a close-up of students intent on discovery (the lights are a Luke Hughes & Company design); a graphic image of the subtle Chinese character of the Keystone library table; a view of one of the study and storage areas.

ABOVE The Scholars' Room, a quiet place at the far end of the long, narrow space, designed to support and encourage concentration and contemplation. The print on the wall is of Lu Ban, revered as the Daoist god of builders, contractors and furniture makers, whose name uses the same character as 'Lu-ke'.

OPPOSITE Open screens separate and divide spaces but still allow light and sight to penetrate. Silhouettes of traditional Qing-dynasty seal scripts are projected on to the walls; even the fire extinguishers are housed in elegantly proportioned cabinets.

灭火器

Fire Extinguisher

DINING HALL, NEW COLLEGE, OXFORD

Transformation of functionality, flexibility – and finance

For Luke Hughes – in full flow as he explains the design parameters of the overhaul of the dining hall at New College, Oxford – interior design tends to be seen as all about cushions and curtains. 'What we do is not interior design,' he says. 'It's really about understanding how people inhabit these spaces. The only way I can describe it is social anthropology. Whatever is being done in a building, our thought process focuses on how to do it better. And that's all dependent on this collective lump of stuff we call furniture.'

A more considered definition of interior design includes the function of space planning – and, indeed, encapsulates precisely the intelligent thinking of which Luke speaks. A good interior designer starts with that same understanding of what people do in spaces that Luke proposes. And when it comes to dining halls, particularly those of academic institutions, the three overriding issues that face a designer – of interiors, of furniture or of social anthropology, whichever

definition he or she subscribes to – are functionality, flexibility and finance.

New College, Oxford, is an excellent example of this planning process in action, but it is one of many. Luke Hughes & Company has redesigned dining-hall furniture for, among many other places, Middle Temple, Gray's Inn, Westminster Abbey, Buckingham Palace, the Tower of London, the Prince of Wales's home at Highgrove in Gloucestershire, Yale University, and numerous colleges at both Oxford and Cambridge. 'A dining hall is part of the identity of a college,' says Luke. 'People come in and mix, eat and talk. Serving that social paradigm is what a dining hall does. The principle of gathering everybody together over a meal is absolutely fundamental to the anthropology of the place.'

It is also, in the 21st century, absolutely fundamental to making the place attractive to the out-of-term conference and event trade, whose delegates are far less likely to be comfortable vaulting a table to get to a seat than

BELOW The real story of this dining hall, as indeed is the case with many of the ones refurbished and refurnished by Luke Hughes & Company, is in the tables. The precisely dimensioned turner's working drawing defines details as small as 2 millimetres ($^1/_8$ in.) and is used for handwork – no CNC machinery here. The blank is 'roughed out' to get the basic shape then worked down to the final dimensions with the aid of a precision instrument: a pair of dividers.

OPPOSITE New College, Oxford, is very far from new, having been founded in 1379 by William of Wykeham, who also founded Winchester College, Hampshire, as a sort of 'feeder' school. Fifteen years before this job, Luke Hughes & Company had made a set of Wykeham chairs for the High Table (where the dons, lecturers and college officials sit) with high backs. Note here the turned table leg, which is new under the dark stain.

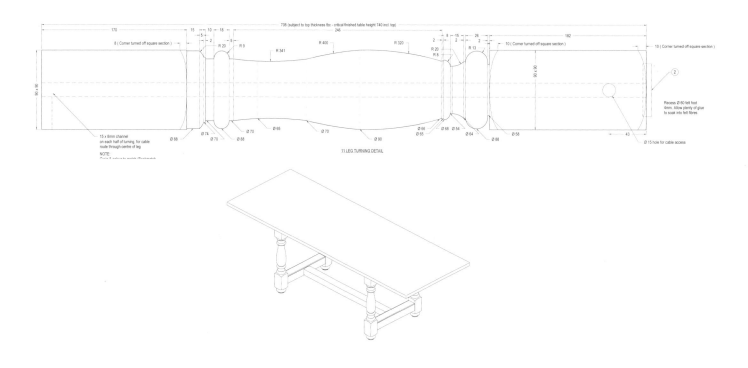

LEFT, TOP AND BOTTOM The knockdown table's assembly and disassembly process is simplicity itself, requiring only a rubber mallet. Stretcher and top rails hook into steel plates recessed into the surfaces that are machined on a taper so the fit becomes tighter as the component settles in. Such design solutions as this enable huge efficiencies, not only of space but also of time; the hall can be cleared of furniture in seventeen minutes. Storage is almost as important as the furniture itself, says Luke. 'We spend as much time designing the storage as we do on the product.'

OPPOSITE The meticulously measured and calculated survey of the New College dining hall (top), detailing four different types of table and top: existing, with no change to the bases, and tops to be trimmed to standard sizes; existing tops with existing but reconfigured bases; existing tops with new demountable bases; and entirely new tables, with new tops and new demountable bases. Through equally careful measuring and dimensioning of tops and legs, so that no sitter found a leg in his or her way, the seating capacity was raised from 184 to 209, 15 per cent more than existing – a boon for the catering department's finances. The image below shows standard-height Wykeham chairs against a table with an existing base and a refurbished top.

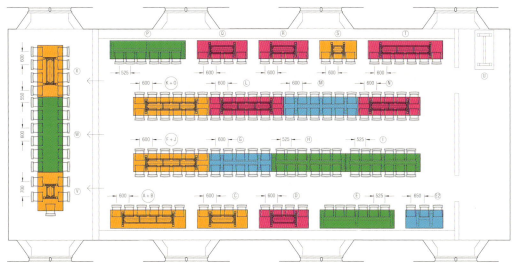

New stacking chair - design TBC

Existing tables (no change to bases, existing tops to be trimmed to standardised dims.)

Existing table tops with reconfigured existing bases (existing tops to be trimmed to standardised dims.)

Existing table tops with new demountable bases (existing tops to be trimmed to standardised dims.)

New tables (to include new tops and new demountable bases)

NOTE:

To seat,
- 184 on Dining Hall main floor
- 25 on Dais
TOTAL CAPACITY: 209 (120% compared to existing seating capacity)

Finished seat spacing subject to state of tables and woodworkers ability to salvage/refurbish once they are at workshop TBC.

LUKE HUGHES & COMPANY
FURNITURE DESIGNERS

CLIENT   NEW COLLEGE, OXFORD - DINING HALL
PROJECT   PROPOSED TABLE & SEATING SCHEME
STATUS   For information

DRAWING NO.   18098/01/005

MATERIALS   N/A
FINISH   N/A
QUANTITY   N/A

OPPOSITE A 'carver' version of the
higher-backed Wykeham chair for
the High Table, next to a bust of the
philosopher Alic Halford Smith, warden
of New College and vice chancellor of
the University of Oxford from 1954–57.
The carved oval in the top back rail of
the chair is of William of Wykeham's
bishop's mitre.

RIGHT Family resemblance: elevations
and sections of the two versions of the
Wykeham chair, manufactured fifteen
years apart, showing construction details.

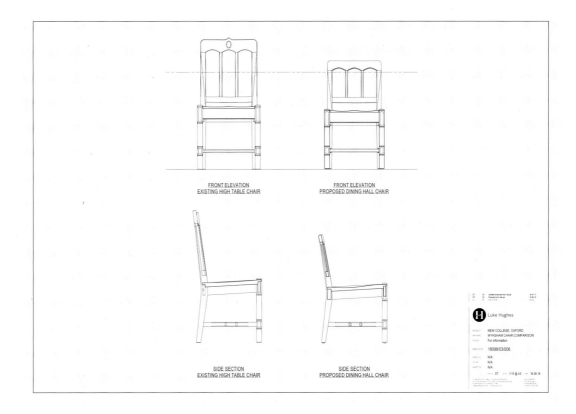

undergraduates were in Luke's day. The familiar need
for flexibility – furniture must be easily and efficiently
reconfigured, rearranged or even removed entirely and
unobtrusively stored for a concert, a wedding or a play –
is very much a part of this same commercial imperative.
'What is interesting', says Luke, 'is that the driver of all
these dining-hall projects has been increasing revenue.

'The first big dining hall we did was in Middle
Temple in the early 1990s. We learnt a lot. Despite it
being in the nature of the great hotels to sell themselves
on their ability to host big events, the truth is that we
are blessed with many "heritage halls", and people
love to dine in a historic or dramatic environment.

'What is also interesting is that the people who now
run the catering operations in university colleges have
come out of the hotel trade. They know about time
efficiency in ways that conventional college catering staff
rarely did. How long it takes to clear two hundred chairs
or rearrange forty tables is vital to the economics. They
train up staff to do it efficiently and put stopwatches on
it. Here, our process enables a hall manager to clear the
space in seventeen minutes, a far cry from four hours.
It saves labour, time and expense – time and again.

'It's also true that squeezing 30 per cent more seats
into a hall – as we did, for instance, at Trinity Hall,

Cambridge – simply by redesigning the positions of the
table legs, transforms the economics of the catering.
It's not just for the twenty-four weeks a year of university
terms; it's working all year round.'

At Trinity Hall, many of the table tops had split
because metal straps had been used to join the solid-oak
planking without allowing for movement of the timber,
and the High Table stretchers were in the wrong place.
'We took all the tables back to the workshop,' says Luke,
'and knocked them apart and cleaned down all the tops,
which are of beautiful, perfectly good oak. We re-cut
mortises, scarfed joints and re-turned stretchers to get
the legs in the right places. We found places to put the
storage racks we designed for all the legs and rails –
we spend as much time designing the storage as we
do on the product. No one sees it, but it's one of the
things that make all the difference.'

For the New College dining hall, where Luke Hughes
& Company had supplied a high-back version of the
Wykeham chair for the High Table fifteen years before,
the work started with detailed surveys. 'There was a
whole series of different tables, most of them Victorian,
plus some really nice ones that look Jacobean but are
in fact from the 1720s, and of course a whole disparate
collection of legs with the gaps in all the wrong places.

OPPOSITE AND BELOW Views of the interior, demonstrating the 'rhythm of quantity' about which Luke Hughes is so passionate. The lamps are a new design by Luke Hughes & Company, on taller stands so diners can see each other across the table, and casting light through the spun-aluminium shades as well as pooling it below. The brass stands are 'slightly Gothic Revival', to pick up the texture of the linenfold panelling on the walls.

OVERLEAF Functional, flexible and financially sound – the three overriding issues that face the designer of dining halls are all admirably served in the New College installation. William of Wykeham, politician, architect, church dignitary and one of the richest men in 14th-century England, approves from his framed and bordered portrait.

We did a survey, plotting the exact position of every single table in the whole hall, then plotted how many seats we could get in, with chairs plus the benches along the wall. We said, if we just put in new chairs we can seat 182, but if we work on the tables as well, refinishing the existing tops and reconfiguring or renewing the bases, and putting in some entirely new tables, we can get it up to 209. That's a significant increase, 15 per cent.

'The demountable knockdown-table system works very well. The top and lower rails and the reconfigured leg frames all come apart with nothing more than a rubber hammer. No hinges, no mechanisms, just stainless-steel hooks that click into plates on the components.

'The other problem was the fixed table lamps. They were so low that you sat looking at the light and couldn't see the person opposite. We designed a new lamp that gives a really good spread of light, with a slightly Gothic Revival brass stand to pick up the linenfold panelling on

the walls. The light comes through the spun-aluminium shade as well as pooling on the table surface itself.

'All this was built up over a three-year period. The work and the relationship is based on the fact that we've been working at New College on and off for twenty-five years. They are very much of the view that if you do these things right then you only do them once, and that will see you through for the next hundred years. They don't mind spending the money with that long-term view.'

Such relationships start with an initial brief. But in almost all cases, says Luke, 'if we designed strictly to the briefs that clients give us, the jobs would never get off the ground. You have to challenge the brief, see how much farther it can go. At Trinity Hall, for instance, the question was, "What can you do for us?" and the answer, as always, was, "We'll really look at it in detail and then come back with what we can do for you." You can invariably push it much further than the client expects.'

BIBLIOGRAPHY

Blakesley, Rosalind P., *The Arts and Crafts Movement* (London: Phaidon, 2006)

Brown, Elizabeth Mills, *New Haven: A Guide to Architecture and Urban Design* (New Haven, CT: Yale University Press, 1976)

Carruthers, Annette, *Edward Barnsley and His Workshop: Arts and Crafts in the Twentieth Century* (Oxford: White Cockade, 1992)

Carruthers, Annette, Mary Greensted and Barley Roscoe, *Ernest Gimson: Arts & Crafts Designer and Architect* (New Haven, CT: Yale University Press, 2019)

Chinnery, Victor, *Oak Furniture: The British Tradition*, rev. edn (Woodbridge: Antique Collectors' Club, 2016)

Crawford, Matthew B., *The Case for Working with Your Hands; or, Why Office Work is Bad for Us and Fixing Things Feels Good* (London: Penguin, 2009)

Dormer, Peter, *The Culture of Craft: Status and Future*, Studies in Design and Material Culture (Manchester: Manchester University Press, 1997)

Farleigh, John (ed.), *Fifteen Craftsmen on Their Crafts* (London: Sylvan Press, 1945)

Greenhalgh, Paul, *Quotations and Sources on Design and the Decorative Arts*, Studies in Design and Material Culture (Manchester: Manchester University Press, 1993)

Greensted, Mary, *Gimson and the Barnsleys: 'Wonderful Furniture of a Commonplace Kind'* (Wolfeboro Falls, NH: Alan Sutton, 1991)

Harrod, Tanya, *The Crafts in Britain in the Twentieth Century* (New Haven, CT: Yale University Press for the Bard Graduate Center for Studies in the Decorative Arts, 1999)

Harvie, Christopher, Graham Martin and Aaron Scharf (eds), *Industrialisation and Culture, 1830–1914* (London: Macmillan for the Open University Press, 1970)

Hughes, Luke, *Furniture Factors: Designing Around the Materials – Brief Technical Considerations for Architects, Specifiers and Designers* (London: Luke Hughes & Company, 1999)

Hughes, Luke, 'Craft's Place in Post-Brexit Britain', *Crafts*, November/December 2017

Leigh, Ray, *Advance the Product: Gordon Russell Furniture – A Continuing Adventure, 1946–1986* (Broadway: Gordon Russell Trust, 2015)

MacCarthy, Fiona, *The Simple Life: C. R. Ashbee in the Cotswolds* (London: Lund Humphries, 1981)

MacCarthy, Fiona, *William Morris: A Life for Our Time* (London: Faber, 2010)

MacCarthy, Fiona, *Anarchy and Beauty: William Morris and His Legacy, 1860–1960* (London: National Portrait Gallery, 2014)

Mason, Anna, *et al.*, *May Morris: Arts & Crafts Designer* (London: Thames & Hudson in association with the Victoria and Albert Museum, 2017)

Morris, William, *The Collected Works of William Morris, with Introductions by His Daughter May Morris*, 24 vols (London: Longmans, Green & Company, 1910–15)

Morris, William, *News from Nowhere, and Other Writings*, ed. Clive Wilmer (London: Penguin, 1993)

Myerson, Jeremy, *Gordon Russell: Designer of Furniture, 1892–1992* (London: Design Council for Gordon Russell Ltd, 1992)

Peters, Alan, *Cabinetmaking: The Professional Approach* (London: Stobart, 1984)

Pevsner, Nikolaus, Pevsner Architectural Guides: Buildings of England (London: Yale University Press)

Pevsner, Nikolaus, *Studies in Art, Architecture, and Design*, 2 vols (London: Thames & Hudson, 1968)

Platman, Lara, *Art Workers Guild: 125 Years – Craftspeople at Work Today* (Norwich: Unicorn Press, 2009)

Pye, David, *The Nature and Art of Workmanship* (London: Cambridge University Press, 1968)

Pye, David, *The Nature and Aesthetics of Design* (London: Barrie & Jenkins, 1978)

Ruskin, John, *The Seven Lamps of Architecture* (London: Smith, Elder & Co., 1849)

Ruskin, John, *The Stones of Venice*, 3 vols (London: Smith, Elder & Co., 1851–53)

Russell, Gordon, *Designer's Trade: Autobiography of Gordon Russell* (London: Allen & Unwin, 1968)

Sennett, Richard, *The Craftsman* (London: Penguin, 2009)

Thompson, Paul, *The Work of William Morris*, 3rd rev. edn (Oxford: Oxford University Press, 1993)

Walker, Aidan, *The Ecology of the Soul: A Manual of Peace, Power and Personal Growth for Real People in the Real World* (Winchester: O Books, 2016)

Walker, Aidan (ed.), *The Encyclopedia of Wood: A Tree-by-Tree Guide to the World's Most Versatile Resource* (Oxford: Facts on File, 1989)

ACKNOWLEDGMENTS

LUKE HUGHES

My immediate thanks go to Aidan Walker, fellow alumnus, fellow author, fellow woodworker and one of the few contemporary design writers who, in modern parlance, 'gets it'. Also, my thanks to Peter Dawson, the book's designer, and, at Thames & Hudson, project editor Mark Ralph and commissioning editor Julian Honer.

There is always a 'behind the scenes' part to any story. In this case, it includes those who have inspired and influenced, those who have advised, early clients who have shown faith, architects who have shared values, designers who have interpreted ideas, craftsmen who helped those ideas materialize. Also, those who, like Tim Imrie, have helped record them over nearly forty years.

Special mention must go to Ray Leigh, Philip Dowson, Philip and Philippa Powell, Mike Johnson, as well as to other designers not mentioned in the text: Ron Carter (my erstwhile Covent Garden neighbour and regular visitor), Jane Dillon, Robin and Lucienne Day, and two people who became friends and were probably the most outstanding craftsmen of their generation, Alan Peters and Martin Grierson.

Thanks, also, to two organizations whose members have had a profound influence: the Artists Rifles Association (founded 1860) and the Art Workers' Guild (1884), both of which conjure from their past and present (and doubtless future) memberships extraordinary talent, ingenuity, courage, creativity and achievement. Long may they thrive.

The company has benefited from various tax incentives for investors in small companies, but nevertheless key shareholders have continued to invest in the business, in particular Richard Walduck, Ian Irvine, Ian Hannam, Andrew Cullen and my siblings and their partners, Kim and Anna Nasmyth, and Jessica and Robin Lough.

Various non-executive directors have offered wise counsel, notable among them Nicholas Mather, Ted Horton and John Price. The greatest debt, in this regard, goes to Charles Breese, who, in 1985, saw potential in some of my wilder idealism, guided the company through three major recessions, and served as a non-executive director for thirty-four years, until 2019. It is hard to know how to even begin to acknowledge the debt.

The client list opposite speaks for itself – all have provided astonishing opportunities. Some provided early breaks, before any reputation was established, and are due special mention, in particular David Gordon-Lennox, Adrian Bridgewater, John Gloag, Dame Jessica Rawson, Dr John Seagrave, David and Suzie Sainsbury and Malcolm Mackenzie.

Of the outstanding team at Luke Hughes, many of whom are pictured on these pages, all have played a crucial part, especially David Snell, Akhter Khalfey and Stephen Sharp, members of the team for nearly thirty years. A monumental debt is owed to Polly Phipps, my formidable companion and toughest critic, who joined the team in 1992, being 'mildy curious about small businesses'. Neither of us could know that, within two years, we would be married. None of this would have been possible without her wisdom, vision, patience, counsel, skill, humour, tolerance and love.

SELECTED CLIENTS

PLACES OF LEARNING

All Souls College, Oxford
Balliol College, Oxford
Bedford School
Benenden School
Brasenose College, Oxford
Broadstone Academy, Shenzhen
Cambridge Botanic Institute
Cambridge University Library
Cambridge University Old Schools
Cambridge University Press
Cambridge University Union Society
Campion Hall, Oxford
Charterhouse School
Christ Church, Oxford
Christ's College, Cambridge
Churchill College, Cambridge
City of London School
Clare College, Cambridge
Corpus Christi College, Cambridge
Corpus Christi College, Oxford
Cranleigh School
Darwin College, Cambridge
Downing College, Cambridge
Duke University
Dyson Centre for Engineering, Cambridge
Emmanuel College, Cambridge
Epsom College
Eton College
Francis Holland School
Gonville & Caius College, Cambridge
Green College, Oxford
Haberdashers' Aske's School
Harrow School
Harvard University
Highgate School
Hughes Hall, Cambridge
Hurstpierpoint College
Institute of Criminology, Cambridge
Jesus College, Cambridge
Jesus College, Oxford
Keble College, Oxford
Keystone Academy, Beijing
King's College, Cambridge

King's College, London
Lincoln College, Oxford
Liverpool Hope University
London School of Economics
Merton College, Oxford
Murray Edwards College, Cambridge
New College, Oxford
Newnham College, Cambridge
Nuffield College, Oxford
Oundle School
Oxford Centre for Hebrew Studies
Pembroke College, Cambridge
Pembroke College, Oxford
Peterhouse, Cambridge
Rhodes House, Oxford
Robinson College, Cambridge
Rodean School
Royal Academy of Music
Royal Grammar School, Guildford
St Anne's College, Oxford
St Antony's College, Oxford
St Catharine's, Cambridge
St Cross College, Oxford
St Edmund Hall, Oxford
St Edmund's College, Cambridge
St Hugh's College, Oxford
St John's College, Cambridge
St John's College, Oxford
St Paul's Girls' School
St Paul's School
St Peter's College, Oxford
Sherborne School
Shrewsbury School
Sidney Sussex College, Cambridge
Stowe School
The Hill School, Pottstown, PA
The King's School, Canterbury
The Queen's College, Oxford
Trinity College, Cambridge
Trinity College, Oxford
Trinity Hall, Cambridge
University College, London
University College, Oxford
University of Birmingham
University of Dundee

University of Edinburgh
University of Liverpool
University of Middlesex
University of Warwick
University of Winchester
Wolfson College, Cambridge
Wolfson College, Oxford
Yale University
Yale-NUS College, Singapore

PLACES OF WORSHIP
Arundel Cathedral
Boxgrove Priory
Bristol Cathedral
Canterbury Cathedral
Cathedral of the Incarnation,
  Garden City, NY
CBST Synagogue, NYC
Chapel of the Resurrection,
  Valparaiso University
Charterhouse School Chapel
Chichester Cathedral
Clare College Chapel, Cambridge
Community Synagogue of Rye, NY
Congregation Habonim, NYC
Derby Cathedral
Dorchester Abbey
Ely Cathedral
Epsom College Chapel
Exeter Cathedral
Guards' Chapel, London
Hereford Cathedral
Hull Minster
Hurstpierpoint College Chapel
Keble College Chapel, Oxford
Mucknell Abbey
Newcastle Cathedral
Park Avenue Synagogue, NYC
Portsmouth Cathedral
Rochester Cathedral
Royal Military Chapel, London
St Albans Cathedral
St Andrew, Holborn
St Andrew's Church, Alderton
St Andrew's Church, Feniton

St Barnabas Church, Dulwich
St Clement Danes, Westminster
St Dunstan's Church, Mayfield
St George's Chapel, Windsor
St George's Church, Bloomsbury
St George's Church, Bristol
St George's Church, Oakdale
St Giles's Cathedral, Edinburgh
St John's Church, Notting Hill
St John's Church, San Francisco
St Joseph's Church, Hackney
St Machar's Cathedral, Aberdeen
St Mary the Less, Durham
St Mary the Virgin, Oxford
St Mary-le-Bow, Cheapside
St Mary's, Ealing
St Mary's, March
St Matthew's Church, Wilton, CT
St Paul's Cathedral
St Paul's Church, Mill Hill
St Peter ad Vincula, Tower of London
St Peter and St Paul, Uppingham
Salisbury Cathedral
Sheffield Cathedral
Shrewsbury School Chapel
Southwark Cathedral
Synagogue B'nai Jeshurun, NYC
Temple Church, London
Trinity Church, Wall Street, NYC
Trinity Episcopal Cathedral,
  Columbia, SC
United Grand Lodge of England
Westminster Abbey
Westminster Cathedral
Westminster Synagogue
Winchester Cathedral

PLACES OF WORK AND LEISURE
Art Workers' Guild
Athenaeum Club
Beefsteak Club
British Academy
British Council
British Heart Foundation
British Museum

Buckingham Palace
English Heritage
Fitzwilliam Museum
Foreign & Commonwealth Office
Garrick Club
General Medical Council
Geological Society
Gray's Inn
Hampton Court Palace
Holyrood House
House of Commons
Inner Temple
Kew Palace
Lincoln's Inn
London Library
Middle Temple
National Gallery
National Gallery of Scotland
National Maritime Museum
Oxford and Cambridge Club
Paul Mellon Centre, London
Royal Albert Hall
Royal Collection Trust
Royal College of Paediatrics
Royal College of Veterinary
  Surgeons
Royal Geographical Society
Royal Institute of British Architects
Royal Opera House
Royal Scottish Academy
Royal Society of Arts
Scottish Supreme Court
Society of Antiquaries
Somerset House
Special Air Service Regiment
Tate Modern
The Wallace Collection
Theatre Royal, Bury St Edmunds
Trinity Real Estate, NYC
TUC
United Kingdom Supreme Court
Victoria and Albert Museum
Windsor Castle
Worshipful Company of Butchers
Worshipful Company of Carpenters

Worshipful Company of Haberdashers
Worshipful Company of
  Leathersellers
Worshipful Company of Mercers
Worshipful Company of Skinners

ARCHITECTURAL COLLEAGUES
Ahrends, Burton & Koralek
Allies and Morrison
Apicella + Bunton
Architecture Research Office
BDP
BGS Architects
BKSK Architects
Burwell Deakins Architects
Buttress Architects
Caroe Architecture
Centerbrook Architects
David Morley Architects
DBVW Architects
Donald Insall Associates
Eric Parry Architects
Feilden+Mawson
Foster + Partners
Gensler
GMW Architects
HOK
Hopkins Architects
Ian Ritchie Architects
Kohn Pedersen Fox
Murphy Burnham & Buttrick
Níall McLaughlin Architects
Pelli Clarke Pelli Architects
Purcell
RHWL
Richard McElhiney Architects
Robert A. M. Stern Architects
Rogers Architects
Sheppard Robson
Skidmore, Owings & Merrill
Stanton Williams
Swanke Hayden Connell
Voith & Mactavish Architects
Wright & Wright Architects
YRM

PICTURE CREDITS

l = left; r = right; t = top; b = bottom; c = centre

2: Tim Imrie; 4: Tim Imrie; 9 (fig. 1): Luke Hughes; 9 (fig. 2): Luke Hughes; 9 (fig. 3): Luke Hughes; 9 (fig. 4): © National Portrait Gallery, London; 9 (fig. 5): © National Portrait Gallery, London; 10: Luke Hughes & Company; 11: Luke Hughes; 12 (fig. 8): Luke Hughes; 12 (fig. 9): Luke Hughes; 12 (fig. 10): Luke Hughes; 13 (fig. 11): Luke Hughes; 13 (fig. 12): Luke Hughes; 14 (fig. 13): Luke Hughes; 14 (fig. 14): Peter Birt; 14 (fig. 15): Luke Hughes; 14 (fig. 16): Mark Turner; 15: Luke Hughes; 17 (fig. 18): Lucius Cary; 17 (fig. 19): Tim Imrie; 17 (fig. 20): Tim Imrie; 17 (fig. 21): Tim Imrie; 17 (fig. 22): Tim Imrie; 18 (fig. 23): Gordon Russell Trust; 18 (fig. 24): Gordon Russell Trust; 18 (fig. 25): Luke Hughes; 18 (fig. 26): Tim Imrie; 19 (fig. 27): Katharine Dowson; 19 (fig. 28): Architectural Press Archive/RIBA Collections; 19 (fig. 29): Aidan Walker; 20: Tim Imrie; 22 (fig. 31): Tim Imrie; 22 (fig. 32): Tim Imrie; 23: Luke Hughes & Company; 24 (fig. 34): Luke Hughes; 24 (fig. 35): Luke Hughes & Company; 24 (fig. 36): Gordon Russell Trust; 25: Tim Imrie; 26: Luke Hughes; 27: Luke Hughes & Company; 28: Luke Hughes; 29 (fig. 41): Luke Hughes & Company; 29 (fig. 42): Luke Hughes; 29 (fig. 43): Luke Hughes & Company; 29 (fig. 44): Luke Hughes; 30: Tim Imrie; 32l: Luke Hughes & Company; 32r: Andrew Dunsmore; 33: Tim Imrie; 34t: Luke Hughes & Company; 34bl: Tim Imrie; 34br: Tim Imrie; 35: Tim Imrie; 36–37: Tim Imrie; 38t: Luke Hughes & Company; 38b: Luke Hughes & Company; 39t: Andrew Dunsmore; 39b: Tim Imrie; 40: Andrew Dunsmore; 41: Tim Imrie; 43tl: Tim Imrie; 43tr: Tim Imrie; 43bl: Luke Hughes; 43br: Tim Imrie; 44: Luke Hughes & Company; 45: Luke Hughes; 46l: Luke Hughes; 46r: Luke Hughes; 47tl: Luke Hughes; 47tr: Luke Hughes; 47bl: Luke Hughes & Company; 47br: Luke Hughes; 48: Luke Hughes; 49t: Luke Hughes; 49bl: Luke Hughes; 49br: Luke Hughes; 50tl: Luke Hughes; 50tr: Luke Hughes; 51t: Luke Hughes; 51b: Luke Hughes; 52: Luke Hughes; 53: Joe Low; 54t: Joe Low; 54b: Joe Low; 55l: Luke Hughes & Company; 55tr: Sophie Hacker; 55br: Luke Hughes; 56–57: Joe Low; 58l: Luke Hughes; 58r: Luke Hughes; 59: Tim Imrie; 60t: Tim Imrie; 60b: Tim Imrie; 61: Tim Imrie; 62: Tim Imrie; 63: Tim Imrie; 64–65: Tim Imrie; 66: Luke Hughes; 67: Luke Hughes & Company; 68: Luke Hughes; 69: Luke Hughes & Company; 70t: Luke Hughes & Company; 70b: Luke Hughes & Company; 71t: Luke Hughes & Company; 71b: Luke Hughes & Company; 72t: Luke Hughes & Company; 72bl: Luke Hughes; 72br: Luke Hughes; 73: Tim Imrie; 74l: Ely Cathedral (Keith Heppell); 74r: Tim Imrie; 75t: Tim Imrie; 75b: Tim Imrie; 76: Tim Imrie; 77: Tim Imrie; 78l: Luke Hughes; 78r: Luke Hughes; 79: Tim Imrie; 80 (all): Luke Hughes; 81: Luke Hughes & Company; 82: Luke Barton; 83: Tim Imrie; 84t: Tim Imrie; 84b: Tim Imrie; 85: Tim Imrie; 86: Tim Imrie; 87l: Tim Imrie; 87r: Luke Hughes; 88t: Luke Hughes; 88b: Luke Hughes & Company; 89: Tim Imrie; 90t: Luke Hughes; 90b: Luke Hughes; 91t: Luke Barton; 91b: Luke Hughes; 92t: Tim Imrie; 92b: Tim Imrie; 93: Tim Imrie; 95: Tim Imrie; 96: Tim Imrie; 97t: Tim Imrie; 97b: Tim Imrie; 98: Luke Hughes; 99: Elizabeth Fellicella; 100 (all): ARO/Luke Hughes & Company; 101: Luke Hughes & Company; 102t: Elizabeth Fellicella; 102b: Elizabeth Fellicella; 103l: Luke Hughes & Company; 103r: Elizabeth Fellicella; 104–105: Elizabeth Fellicella; 106l: Getty Images/Bettmann Collection; 106r: Luke Hughes; 107: Luke Hughes & Company; 108–109: Rev. Brian Johnson; 110t: Luke Hughes; 110c: Luke Hughes; 110b: Luke Hughes & Company; 111: Luke Hughes & Company; 112: Luke Hughes & Company; 113t: Luke Hughes; 113b: Luke Hughes; 114–15: Rev. Brian Johnson; 116: © Dennis Gilbert/VIEW; 118l: © Peter Cook/VIEW; 118r: © Peter Cook/VIEW; 119: © Peter Cook/VIEW; 120l: Luke Hughes; 120ct: Luke Hughes; 120br: Luke Hughes; 121: © Peter Cook/VIEW; 122t: Tim Imrie; 122bl: Tim Imrie; 122br: Tim Imrie; 123: Tim Imrie; 124: Tim Imrie; 125: Tim Imrie; 126: Tim Imrie; 127tl: Luke Hughes & Company; 127bl: Tim Imrie; 127r: Luke Hughes & Company; 128–29: Tim Imrie; 130l: Tim Imrie; 130r: Tim Imrie; 131t: Luke Hughes & Company; 131b: Luke Hughes & Company; 132tl: Luke Hughes; 132bl: Luke Hughes; 132r: Luke Hughes; 133: Tim Imrie; 134tl: Tim Imrie; 134bl: Tim Imrie; 134br: Luke Hughes; 135l: Tim Imrie; 135r: Tim Imrie; 136t: Tim Imrie; 136b: Tim Imrie; 137l: Tim Imrie; 137r: Tim Imrie; 138–39: © United Kingdom Supreme Court; 140–41: Tim Imrie; 142: Luke Hughes; 143t: Tim Imrie; 143b: Tim Imrie; 144: Tim Imrie; 145: Tim Imrie; 146: Tim Imrie; 147: Tim Imrie; 148: Tim Imrie; 149: Tim Imrie; 150l: © Dennis Gilbert/VIEW; 150r: Luke Hughes; 151:

Page 23 (fig. 33): The Luke Hughes & Company team in July 2018. Back row (from left): Stephen Sharp, Justin Marchant, Dami Babalola, James Woodgate, Josh Beech, Charlotte Smith, Chris Hill, Nicola Murphy, David Snell, Laura Tunstall, Nigel Shepherd, Caroline Maddox, Luke Barton, Julie Brooker, Duncan Taylor and Kathryn Weedon. Front row (from left): Peter Duggan, Julian Thomas, Luke Hughes, Katie Spence and Polly Phipps.

INDEX

Aidan Walker studied history at Cambridge University before working as a furniture designer and cabinetmaker. He subsequently became editor and editorial director of most of the UK's professional design journals, and he regularly chairs design conferences in New York, the Middle East, China and elsewhere. He is the editor of *The Encyclopedia of Wood* (1989), for which Luke Hughes was a contributing writer.

Tanya Harrod is one of today's most respected design historians. Her book *The Crafts of Britain in the Twentieth Century* (1999) won the Historians of British Art book award in 2000.

FRONT COVER The Bradfield chair.

BACK COVER Clockwise from top: the Wykeham chair (see pages 200, 236); detail of bench seat and low table in the Sainsbury Botanic Institute Laboratory, University of Cambridge (see page 202); the Napoleon chair.

PAGE 2 The nave altar at Ely Cathedral (see page 75).

PAGE 4 The Bradfield chair.

Furniture in Architecture: The Work of Luke Hughes – Arts & Crafts in the Digital Age
© 2020 Thames & Hudson Ltd, London

Foreword © 2020 Tanya Harrod

Text © 2020 Aidan Walker

Illustrations © 2020 the copyright holders; see page 250 for details

All images have been reproduced with permission. Any omissions or errors in the picture credits that are brought to the publisher's attention will be rectified in future editions.

Designed by Peter Dawson, gradedesign.com

First published in 2020 in the United States of America by Thames & Hudson Inc., 500 Fifth Avenue, New York, New York 10110

www.thamesandhudsonusa.com

Library of Congress Control Number 2019947908

ISBN 978-0-500-02254-2

Printed and bound in China by Toppan Leefung Printing Limited